INTERCITY 125

R.M. Tufnell

Foulis

Haynes

ISBN 0 85429 428 7

A FOULIS Railway Book

First published 1984

© **Winchmore Publishing Services Ltd 1984**

Published by:
Haynes Publishing Group
Sparkford,
Yeovil,
Somerset BA22 7JJ

Distributed in USA by:
Haynes Publications Inc.
861 Lawrence Drive,
Newbury Park,
California 91320, USA

Produced by:
Winchmore Publishing Services Limited,
40 Triton Square,
London NW1 3HG

Printed in Spain
by Graficromo s.a.

Titles in the *Super Profile* series:

Deltics (F430)
Great Western Kings (F426)
Green Arrow (F427)
Gresley Pacifics (F429)
InterCity 125 (F428)
Royal Scot (F431)

Austin-Healey 'Frogeye'
Sprite (F343)
Ferrari 250GTO (F308)
Fiat X1/9 (F341)
Ford GT40 (F332)
Jaguar E-Type (F370)
Jaguar D-Type & XKSS (F371)
Jaguar Mk 2 Saloons (F307)
Lotus Elan (F330)
MGB (F305)
*MG Midget & Austin-Healey Sprite
(except 'Frogeye') (F344)*
Morris Minor & 1000 (ohv) (F331)
Porsche 911 Carrera (F311)
Triumph Stag (F342)

BSA Bantam (F333)
MV Agusta America (F334)
Norton Commando (F335)
Honda CB750 sohc (F351)
Sunbeam S7 & S8 (F363)
BMW R69 & R69S (F387)

Avro Vulcan (F436)
B29 Superfortress (F339)
Boeing 707 (F356)
de Havilland Mosquito (F422)
Harrier (F357)
Mikoyan-Gurevich MiG 21 (F439)
P51 Mustang (F423)
Phantom II (F376)
Sea King (F377)
SEPECAT Jaguar (F438)
Super Etendard (F378)
Tiger Moth (F421)
Bell UH-1 Iroquois (F437)

Further titles in this series will be published at regular intervals. For information on new titles please contact your bookseller or write to the publisher.

Contents

InterCity 125 set 2 + 8 formation passing the halfway sign near Tollerton.

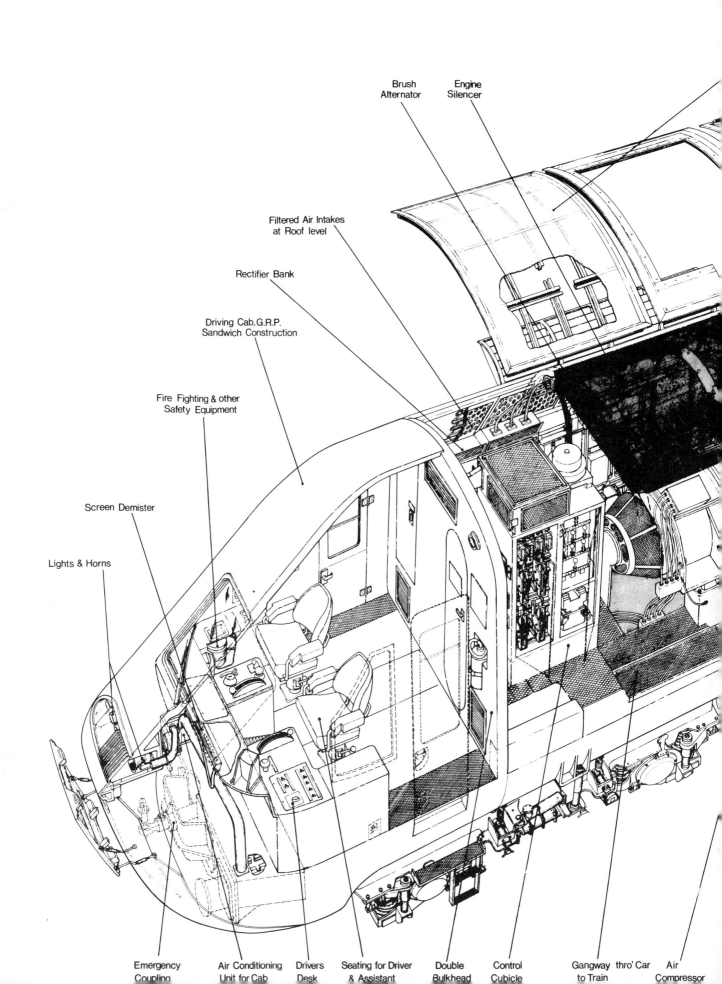

Brush
Alternator

Engine
Silencer

Filtered Air Intakes
at Roof level

Rectifier Bank

Driving Cab, G.R.P.
Sandwich Construction

Fire Fighting & other
Safety Equipment

Screen Demister

Lights & Horns

Emergency
Coupling

Air Conditioning
Unit for Cab

Drivers
Desk

Seating for Driver
& Assistant

Double
Bulkhead

Control
Cubicle

Gangway thro' Car
to Train

Air
Compressor

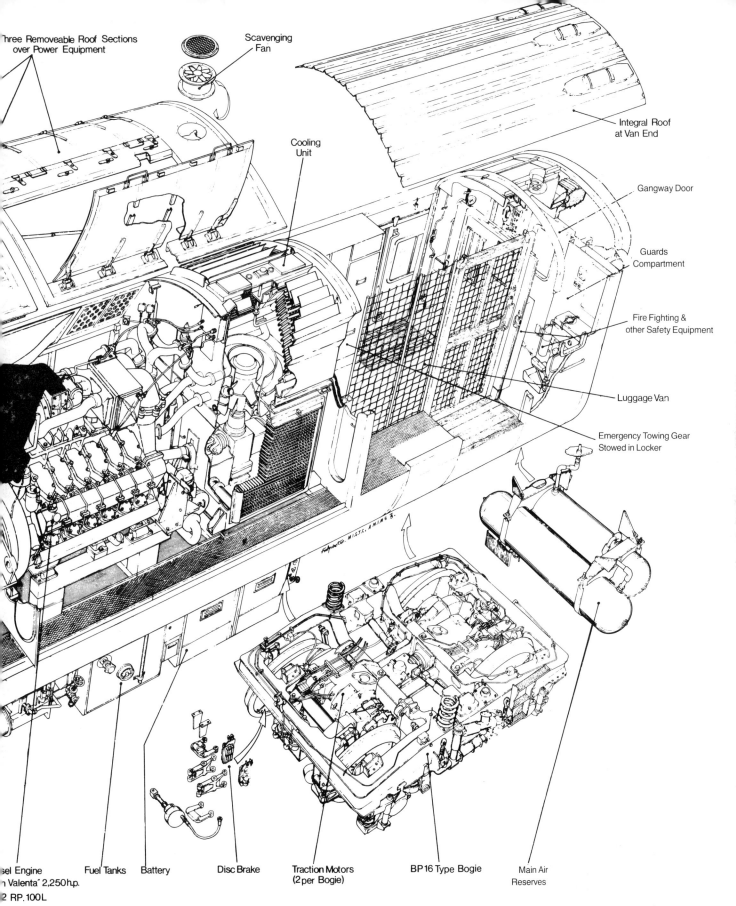

Three Removeable Roof Sections over Power Equipment

Scavenging Fan

Cooling Unit

Integral Roof at Van End

Gangway Door

Guards Compartment

Fire Fighting & other Safety Equipment

Luggage Van

Emergency Towing Gear Stowed in Locker

...sel Engine
...n Valenta˝ 2,250 h.p.
...2 RP.100L

Fuel Tanks

Battery

Disc Brake

Traction Motors (2 per Bogie)

BP 16 Type Bogie

Main Air Reserves

Arrangement of Power Car for High Speed Train

Showing the layout of Power Equipment

Origins

The 'InterCity' network started from a cloud no bigger than a man's hand with one named train on the Western Region of British Railways in 1953. That train ran from London (Paddington) to Birmingham (Snow Hill), now alas no more, leaving London at 9.00 am and returning from Birmingham at 5.00 pm. The true flavour of a footplate journey on this route prior to 1962 is captured on an Argo Transcord record, number EAF 75. In order to get the real effect this should be played in a darkened room at the maximum sound value that the neighbourhood will accept.

The origins of the name go even further back to 1933 when the Southern Railway, following its electrification of the main line to Brighton, ran a 'City Limited' express from Brighton to London Bridge; the service ran at 8.45 am from Brighton and returned from London Bridge at 5.00 pm. The formation was an all-steel 12-car train with Pullman cars and electric kitchens, features later adopted in the luxury Trans European Expresses, but the ride left a lot to be desired — as did all the Southern electric stock.

Just before World War I, the London & North Western Railway was running a service of express trains between London (Euston) and Birmingham (New Street) amounting to 40 trains a day, nine of them non-stop in two hours for the 114 miles (183.5 km). One of these diverted from the main line at the London end of Primrose Hill tunnel and ran along the North London line to Broad Street station, one of the three main line stations actually in the City of London, thereby earning the name 'City to City Limited', but it had only a comparatively short life because of the war.

Following the 1955 Modernisation Plan and Dr Beeching's re-appraisal plans of 1963, the whole main line passenger network was revamped to allow for higher operational speeds using the power available with the new diesel and electric locomotives.

The first main line diesel locomotives entered service in 1958, but the highest powered units at that time were the English Electric Company's diesel-electric 2,000-hp type 4 (later class 40) and the Western Region's 2,000-hp diesel hydraulic 'Warship' class (later class 42). As these had to run in conjunction with steam locomotives and with many speed restrictions on the West Coast main line due to electrification work, the early results from the diesel locomotives were disappointing. There were also considerable problems with the train heating due to the poor quality of the control gear on the train heating boilers installed in the diesel locomotives; sometimes steam locomotives had to be used between the diesels and the train to supply the steam for the train heating in the winter.

To revert to 1955, when the Modernisation Plan was announced, a number of significant events took place which had their effect on the future passenger rail network.

In February came the announcement of a new motorway to be built from London to Yorkshire, to be known as the M1, and in March the French Railways (SNCF) ran a couple of electric locomotives at 205 mph (330 km/h) near Bordeaux to test bogie riding and were horrified by the obvious wear and tear when the bogies were subsequently examined. Then in October the English Electric Company produced their prototype 'Deltic' diesel electric locomotive at a rating of 3300 hp on 106 tons (107,702.8 kg), at that time the most powerful diesel locomotive in the world and capable of speeds up to 105 mph (169 km/h). Lastly in November a decision was made to adopt 25 kV at 50 Hz for all future electrification schemes except on the Southern Region of British Rail, where the DC system was to be retained.

Part of the Modernisation Plan had been the proposed electrification of both East and West Coast main lines, the first to cover the Eastern and North-Eastern Regions (as they were then) from Kings Cross to Leeds and to Newcastle upon Tyne, the other to include the London Midland and the Scottish Regions to Birmingham, Manchester, Liverpool and to Glasgow. Since these schemes could not be achieved simultaneously, the West Coast route was given priority because it carried the heaviest traffic and on 12 September 1960 the first portion of that route from Manchester to Crewe was brought into service. This was followed in January 1962 with electric services from Crewe to Liverpool and on 25 October 1965 the rest of the system from Crewe to Euston was energised for trial running. The full service was opened on 3 January 1966 from Euston to Liverpool and Manchester with 100 mph (161 km/h) operation as far as Rugby, apart from speed restrictions to 80 mph (129 km/h) at Berkhamstead and at Weedon. At that time this gave British Rail the fastest service of high speed trains anywhere in the world, with average speeds of 80 mph (129 km/h), but the East Coast route was left to do its best with diesel locomotives and in 1959 had obtained the prototype Deltic for trials.

It had become obvious to the passenger-operating side that in order to compete with the private motor car for inter-city journeys an average overall speed of at least 75 mph (121 km/h) was essential; and that was before the days of motorways. In order to achieve these average speeds, considerable running at 100 mph (161 km/h) would be necessary with plenty of power in hand for recovery from speed restrictions

The first diesel-hauled 'Cornish Riviera' in June 1958 crossing Brunel's Saltash Bridge.

and signal checks, as well as delays due to permanent way works and maintenance. Part of the 1955 Modernisation Plan had been to refurbish both track and signalling, which had received a bare minimum of essential work since the end of World War II in 1945; at that time (1955) they were only just adequate to cope with the then permitted maximum speed of 90 mph (145 km/h), which was all the first batch of main line diesel locomotives was designed to achieve.

Trials with the Deltic and its 105 mph (169 km/h) capability convinced the Eastern, North Eastern and Scottish Regions that a timetable could be established with track and signalling upgraded to 100 mph (161 km/h) running to produce overall speeds of 75 mph (121 km/h) by the use of a fleet of 22 Deltics; these were ordered in March 1958. That was a few months before both the 'Cornish Riviera' and the 'Flying Scotsman' first went over to diesel haulage.

Production problems meant that the complete fleet of 22 Deltics was not finally delivered until April 1962, in time for the summer services that year.

The first immediate result was a reduction in the running time of the 'Flying Scotsman' from seven hours to six for the 393 miles (632 km) (65 mph/105 km/h), but this had to include speed reductions to 20 mph (32 km/h) at Peterborough, 25 mph (40 km/h) at York, 30 mph (48 km/h) at Durham and Newcastle, 40 mph (64 km/h) at Morpeth and Portobello as well as fourteen others between 45 mph (73 km/h) and 90 mph (145 km/h). The majority of these were not alleviated until 1973.

Another result was the effect of these speeds upon the braking problem. The trial test with the prototype Deltic had shown that stopping from 102 mph (164 km/h) on a downhill stretch of track required 6,219 ft (1,896 m), about 1,000 ft (305 m) more than the signalling system of that time was designed for. This also showed up the weakness of the British vacuum brake system for high speed services, since a similar test

in Germany with air-braked stock only needed 4,490 ft (1,369 m) to stop from 100 mph (161 km/h).

At the time the Modernisation Plan was introduced there were two features that were considered essential by the engineers in the British Transport Commission, namely braking by compressed air and the use of electricity for train heating in place of steam, but they were over-ruled by the Regional General Managers except on the Southern Region, where these features were mostly in use anyway. The retention of the vacuum brake, which for some obscure reason was also used on all the diesel multiple units, meant longer spacing between signals and therefore fewer trains per hour on any particular stretch of track, which in turn affected its earning capacity. Conversely, the retention of the braking distance of 6,660 ft (2,030 m) for 100 mph (161 km/h) operation did mean that the High Speed Train (HST), when it was introduced, could be braked from its top speed of 125 mph (201 km/h) within the existing signalling system by making use of disc brakes without costly resiting of

'Blue Pullman' new ex-works. The Pullman crest was later added to the nose of the power cars.

First class dining car of the Blue Pullman trains – a very pleasant way to travel.

the distant signals.

The possession of the 22 Deltics in conjunction with some of the first 2,750-hp Brush-built D.1500 class (later class 47) gave the East Coast route a considerable advantage in 1962/3 over the West Coast line, then in the throes of electrification and with no diesels more powerful than the 2,500-hp Derby-built 1Co-Co1 'Peak' class (classes 44 and 45). The London Midland Region had been relying heavily on these locomotives to tide them over during the process of electrification, but they suffered from a number of electrical problems and had to be relegated to the former Midland main line from St Pancras to Leicester, Derby and Manchester. The line from Euston was left to be worked by the 2,000-hp class 40 type, supplemented later by some of the Brush class 47s.

Birmingham and Manchester were fortunate in having alternative routes to London and some attempt was made to give these cities a higher-speed service by the use of the 'Blue Pullman' trains, first to Manchester via the Midland line where the original Pullmans were used in 1874, and later to Birmingham, to Bristol and to South Wales. These services were limited to one train a day in each direction and, with a maximum speed of 90 mph

(145 km/h), did not do much to improve the situation. Their riding qualities left a lot to be desired, particularly in the end coaches of each set, though the ride in the driver's cab was superb.

These Blue Pullmans were a fixed-formation train set based on the ideas of the Trans European Expresses, but they were an expensive way of achieving the desired result. That could have been obtained at much less cost by the use of a conventional locomotive with conventional Pullman cars, as was demonstrated by the Eastern Region in their 'Master Cutler' and other Pullman trains. The Blue Pullmans were, however, the first trains in the UK to be equipped with full air conditioning and their basic conception was the same as that subsequently adopted for the High Speed Train.

By 1964, while average speeds on the East Coast line had improved in some cases to over 70 mph (113 km/h) those on the West Coast line had slipped, due to the electrification works, from 58 mph (93 km/h) to 54 mph (87 km/h) for Glasgow and from 51 mph (82 km/h) to 44 mph (71 km/h) for Liverpool, which was the worst affected of all the major cities since it had no alternative route over which any form of speeded-up service could be offered. Apart from the main lines to the North of England and to Scotland, what about the other regions of British Railways, the Western and the Southern? How did they fare under the Modernisation Plan?

The Western Region, true to the Great Western tradition, chose a quite separate course in opting to use hydraulic transmission for their diesel locomotives which were built to German designs modified to suit the British loading gauge. These locomotives were supplied from three sources: their own works at Swindon and two well-known steam locomotive builders, the North British Locomotive Company of Glasgow and Beyer-Peacock of Gorton, Manchester. The decision by the Western Region to use hydraulic transmission was initiated by H.H. Phillips, at that time Assistant General Manager. The design was based on the V.200 locomotives just produced by Krauss-Maffei of Munich, in which an output of 2,000 hp was built on a wheel arrangement B-B at 80 tonnes (80,000 kg) by the use of a body of stressed skin on a light tubular chassis. This design involved the use of two high speed (1,500 rpm) diesel engines and, though the weight saved should have given extra haulage capacity, this was largely offset by much higher running resistance; further, the electrical control equipment was almost as elaborate as that in a diesel-electric locomotive. They also suffered from lack of braking capacity when hauling unbraked freight trains, which their German counterparts were not called on to do, and the periods between overhauls were very much shorter than those for the diesel electrics, certainly those with medium speed diesel engines.

When the time came to produce a 2,700-hp version, the hydraulic design proved no lighter than its electric equivalent but a lot more expensive both in first cost and in maintenance. Finally, when both the North British and Beyer-Peacock firms went out of business, and the pound had slipped against the Deutschmark, the maintenance problems proved insuperable and by 1977 all the diesel hydraulics had been withdrawn.

In spite of these problems the Western Region did make some considerable improvements in their passenger train speeds; they restored the 'Bristolian' to its pre-war 100 minute timing and improved speeds to the West of England and South Wales.

Average speeds of 70 mph (113 km/h) were achieved to Newport and to Taunton, while 75 mph (121 km/h) could be obtained to Chippenham; but the nature of the lines west of Exeter and beyond Newport precluded higher average speeds than 60 mph (97 km/h) to Cardiff and to Plymouth. Later, the use of two class 42 locomotives, giving 4,400 hp and weighing 156 tons (158,505 kg) enabled a nine-coach train weighing just 330 tons (335,301 kg) to be run to Exeter at 74 mph (119 km/h) and to Plymouth at 64 mph (103 km/h). Although the power and weight of the latter combination was not far short of that for the future HST, the overall performance was not comparable.

Lastly the Southern Region pursued its own course of steady expansion of its DC-electrified system and by 1962 had eliminated steam working in all sections except the former London & South Western main line. That region had made some trials with 1,760-hp and 2,000-hp diesel-electrics from 1951 to 1955, but preferred to stay with its rebuilt Bulleid Pacifics until the electrification to Southampton and Bournemouth which was achieved in 1967.

High overall speeds are not a feature of the Southern Region and even now the best times to Southampton and Bournemouth only produce overall averages of 68 mph (109 km/h) and 66 mph (106 km/h) respectively, while the next best is 54 mph (87 km/h) to Brighton. Fortunately for British Rail, a lack of motorways in that area and the problems of parking in London do not make the motor car such a serious competitor in the matter of speed as on the other side of the Thames.

The result of all this, combined with the beginning of the motorway system and the disastrous drivers' strike of 1955, was a steady loss of passenger business, and some forcible action was necessary to counter this. New steps had to be taken in order to further improve operating speeds.

Coaching Stock Developments

One of the first effects of the higher speed schedules introduced from about 1962 was to show up the poor riding qualities of the standard Mk I coach bogies then in general use, although a certain amount of swaying, combined with spilled coffee in the restaurant car, was generally accepted as part of a fast train ride and the seating was softer and more comfortable than nowadays. The Mk I coach had been brought out soon after nationalisation and the bogie design was based on pre-war standards. The best of the pre-war coach bogies had been the Gresley model on the LNER, but they were expensive to build and maintain. The Mk I design was based on the use of laminated springs and axle boxes located in hornguides, which were prone to wear. The suspension links which took the body load also had knife edge supports which wore; the combination of these factors produced a ride which was most unsatisfactory at much over 60 mph (97 km/h).

Improvements in private automobile suspensions and a generally higher level of transport comfort meant that something had to be done about the vehicle ride

qualities. Before the 1923 amalgamation, the best riding coaches had been fitted with three axle bogies which gave a magnificent ride, but these had all been phased out in the late 1920s and would have been too expensive to build. The first attempts at bogie improvement had been the use of the Commonwealth cast steel framed bogie, but these were heavier and more expensive; they also suffered from the same basic faults as the Mk I bogie.

Meanwhile the same problems were being experienced in Europe and the UIC (Union Internationale de Chemin de Fer) had come up with the design of a bogie employing coil springs with the axle-boxes located by a swinging arm. A redesigned version of that bogie was introduced on British Railways as the Mk IV bogie and gave an enormous improvement to the ride and to the maintenance problem. This was incorporated into the Mk II passenger coach and these began to come into service

Train of Mk I coaching stock hauled by class 42 diesel-hydraulic locomotive near Reading.

in 1963 for the first of the InterCity trains introduced on the East Coast route to Newcastle upon Tyne.

In 1964 the Research Department at Derby was provided with new test and development facilities and the problem of ride control was immediately tackled. The most immediate problem concerned the suspension of the non-bogie freight wagon, which had for long been the bane of the UK railway system. Britain was almost the only country still operating trains made up of four-wheel wagons with loose couplings and without brakes. The overall operating speeds of these trains was around 4 mph (6.5 km/h) with a maximum of 40 mph (65 km/h) on the main line. This impeded efforts to introduce higher speeds because the super elevation of the track on bends could not be raised above these levels of speed in case

Mk II coach. The first application of the new B.4 bogie.

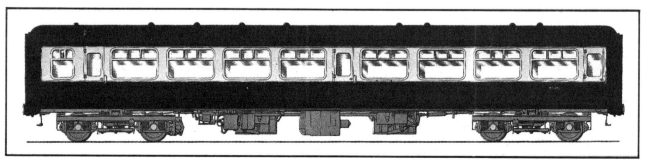

the train had to be stopped on a bend. Also the axle-boxes would not stand sustained speeds even of 40/45 mph (65/72 km/h) as the Southern Region found when they put their Co-Co electric locomotives onto freight operation; those locomotives could sustain these speeds uphill and downhill which was more than the freight vehicle bearings would take and caused numerous hot boxes in service.

In the Research Laboratory at Derby Mr A.H. Wickens found that the major problem was to overcome vehicle hunting – sideways oscillations which were the real limitation to high speed running. The problem of differential action between the two ends of a rigid wheel and axle had traditionally been overcome by turning the tyre tread to a taper, so that on bends the outer wheel ran on a larger diameter than the inner one. This caused hunting when running on straight track and, on the pre-war LNER streamlined

trains, the tyres on the last bogie of the special 'Beaver tail' observation car were turned parallel to counter this problem. In the new Derby-designed freight vehicle a completely novel

Interior view of the Derby Research Laboratory with space-framed APT in the background.

An experimental APT on trials. This version was driven by Leyland gas turbines.
Inset Bogie for the Advanced Passenger Train with a power car in the background.

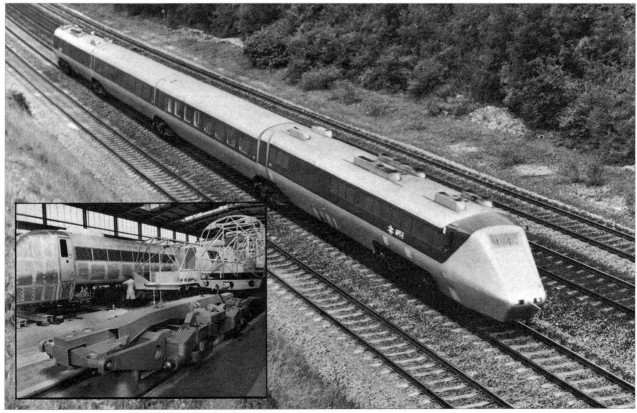

Mk III coach with B.5 bogie and full air conditioning.
Mk III coach interior, first class.
Mk III coach interior, second class.

suspension system was used as well as a new profile of tyre tread. The new system allowed some measure of steering round bends and was so successful that speeds of up to 100 mph (161 km/h) on the track and of 140 mph (225 km/h) on test rollers in the laboratory were able to be obtained. These findings were then applied to a passenger vehicle bogie which showed that operation at up to 155 mph (250 km/h) could be satisfactorily obtained in service, but then the problem was how to make use of this capability in service operation. There were two possibilities: either to build completely new lines – the option adopted by Japan and France – or to try to run on the existing layout; the latter

would involve the use of a tilt mechanism to get round all the curves in our existing system without too much reduction in speed. It was estimated that the journey time from London to Glasgow (401 miles/645 km) would be 270 minutes (89 mph/143 km/h) without assisted tilt or 220 minutes (109 mph/175 km/h) using a 9° tilt.

By 1966, when the InterCity service network was firmly established, the railways' share of the passenger traffic over the whole country for journeys of over one hundred miles was 14 per cent, compared to 77 per cent by private car and the ownership of private cars at that date was just over 9.5 million. The percentage of passenger traffic on the route

between London and Manchester had increased from 59.3 per cent in 1965 to 70 per cent in 1966 as a result of the electrification, which showed what could be achieved by the provision of a good service of fast, regular interval trains.

Conceived in 1967, authorisation to proceed with the building of an experimental Advanced Passenger Train was given in 1969, using the tilting principle; the first prototype (APT-E) was built using gas turbines for propulsion and this was ready for trials in July 1972.

Long before this however it became obvious to Mr T.C.B. Miller MBE, then Chief Mechanical and Electrical Engineer at the British Railways Board, that the APT

Mk III coaches under construction at
Litchurch Lane works, Derby.

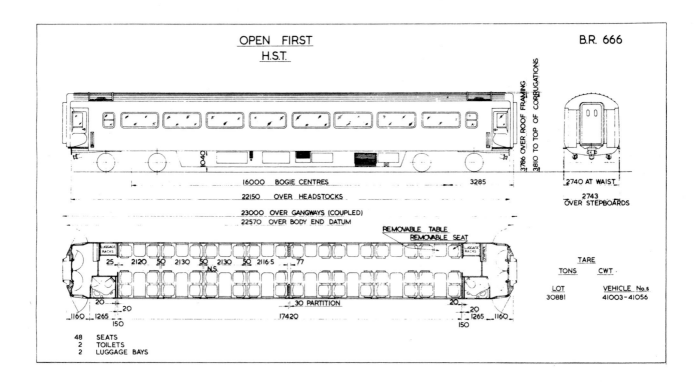

Coach layout. Open first class.

Coach layout. Open second class.

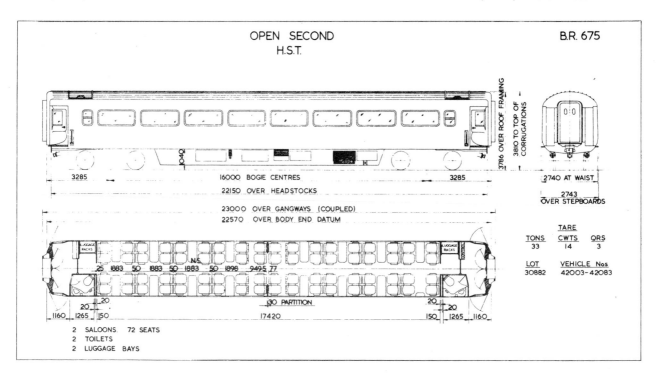

would not provide the nationwide high speed service required in time to meet the competition from an ever increasing number of private automobiles and an expanding network of motorways. As a result a completely new concept of high speed train was drawn up using conventional components, including high speed diesel engines for propulsion and disc brakes for stopping and which could be built to an axle load of 17 tons (17,273 kg); that was the most that the Civil Engineer would allow for operation at the proposed speed of 125 mph (201 km/h). The speed chosen was a combination of the most that the signalling system would permit for the braking distances obtainable, the best that the track could be improved to take and the most that the available power units would

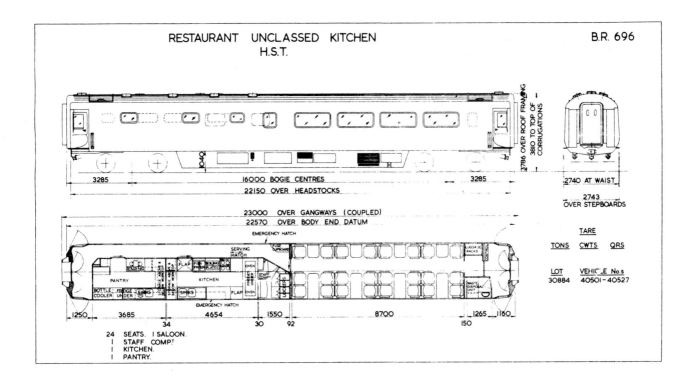

Coach layout. Kitchen car.

Coach layout. Buffet car.

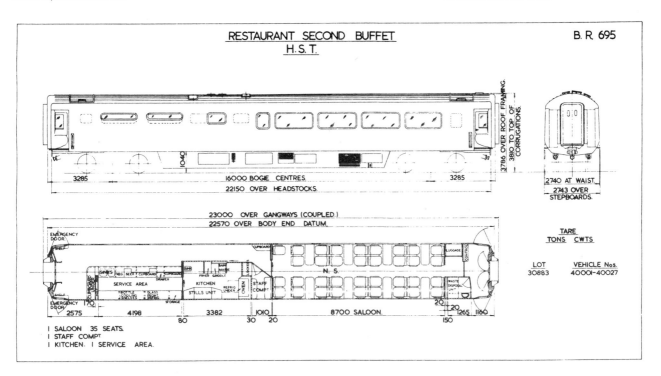

give within the weight limitations imposed. At first there was some confusion among officials of the BR Board, who thought that this was an alternative APT using diesel engines; but when all that was sorted out, this project was authorised late in 1969 as well, and

the first prototype train, called the HST-125, was completed by June 1972.

When the Mk IIb coaching stock was introduced in 1965 there was a vast improvement in ride resulting from the use of the new B.5 bogie, which employed coil spring

suspension allied to axle-boxes located by radius arms. It made the 100 mph (161 km/h) operation on the East and West Coast lines, as well as on the Western lines to South Wales and the West of England, a really pleasurable occasion. Prior to the introduction of this stock a complete train of eight experimental coaches called Project XP 64 had been built and sent around the country for evaluation. This embodied a number of new features such as extra-wide folding doors, double glazed windows, pressure ventilation with much better sound-proofing and lighting. The second class accommodation was all in saloon type coaches, but for the first class passenger separate compartments were still retained. There were fold-up tables and magazine racks in each seat back which was made of fibreglass. Most of these features were retained in the Mk IIb stock except the wide folding doors (which had proved troublesome in service), the folding tables and the magazine racks. The Mk IIb stock was 66 feet (20 m) long and designed to operate at up to 100 mph (161 km/h).

When the higher speeds of the APT and the HST were proposed it was obvious that a new and improved design of coach was going to be required; it would have to incorporate full air conditioning, automatic doors between coaches, an improved vestibule connection and much stronger integral construction to withstand operation at 125 mph (201 km/h) or more. This would of course have to include the possible results of a derailment at high speed and so the present Mk III stock was born, used for both the InterCity 125 and for locomotive-hauled trains on other high speed routes. The coaching stock for the APT was a completely different concept since that had to be much lighter in weight and be capable of tilting through 9° while still remaining within the loading gauge.

The bogies for the Mk III stock are an improvement on the B.5, employing secondary air suspension and disc brakes and known as the BT.10 type. The coach length is increased to 75 feet (23 m) overall and is built up using rolled steel sections with a stressed skin, all-steel body and a ribbed steel roof. Buckeye couplings are fitted and the vestibule gangways, of skimmed foam construction, are attached to the couplers so that they are always in line even on a tight curve.

Each coach has wide-hinged entrance doors at each end and the sliding doors separating the vestibule from the seating area are automatically operated by treadmats in the approach floor area. This can be a source of annoyance if children are allowed to rush up and down the coach opening the doors at each end until someone protests.

The interior panels are located by clip-in fastenings so that they can be removed for maintenance of pipework and wiring, and for replacement by more up-to-date designs if fashions change. Before these are fitted the whole coach is treated with bitumen-based sound-deadening compound so that a sound level of 65 decibels (dBa) is achieved at 125 mph (201 km/h); this compares with 77 dBa for Mk I stock at 90 mph (145 km/h) and with 69 dBa for Mk II stock also at 90 mph (145 km/h).

Saloon type bodies are used for both first and second class accommodation. The seats and tables are secured to rails running the length of the coach and the first class seats have individual adjustment. The first class layout gives 48 seats – two one side and one the other of the central walkway. As there are eight windows each side, each pair of first class seats has a window. In the second class 72 seats are provided, two each side of the walkway so that the seats do not correspond exactly to the windows. The fixed armrest between the two seats makes access to the window-side seat awkward where tables are fitted.

The seats, which many people think are not as comfortable as those in the earlier Mk I stock, were designed by a 'panel of medical, ergonomic and industrial design experts' – so that accounts for it! The seat covers are removable for cleaning when necessary.

Since the bodyside windows are sealed, double-glazed units (tinted to reduce glare) a controlled system of ventilation is required, combined with heating and cooling facilities, and this service is provided by an air conditioning module mounted below the floor in each coach. This is designed to maintain an air temperature of 21°C (plus or minus 2°) with outside ambient temperatures between −6°C and 28°C. The lighting is by fluorescent fittings in roof-mounted diffusers and is designed to produce a minimum of 25 lumens at all seats.

Underfloor modules, separately removable for maintenance, are supplied with electricity from the main engines and control the brakes, the air conditioning and the batteries which supply these services if the main engines are not running.

Catering facilities consist basically of two types. First, a kitchen car occupying half a coach, with seating for 24 places in the other half, and the ability to supply 120 passengers with full meal service in two adjacent cars. Secondly, a buffet car with seating for 35 places, providing a take away service for passengers to consume either in the buffet car or to take back to their own seats. There is also a design for a third type of combined kitchen and buffet car which could provide 42 full meals as well as the take away service of the straight buffet car, but so far this has not yet been built.

Significantly this Mk III coaching stock was due to be produced just about the time that the design of the High Speed Train was being formulated and while it was not suitable for the APT it was suitably modified for use in the HST or InterCity 125 as it was to be known.

254.025 set InterCity 125 between Edinburgh and Newcastle.

InterCity 125 unit on a Torbay-bound summer holiday train, passing Shell Cove between Dawlish and Teignmouth on 30 July 1983.

Mk III coach colour scheme.

Cutaway view of a Mk III coach showing components and bogie.

Unit 253.010 heads a Plymouth-Paddington express up to Dainton Summit on 9 September 1980.

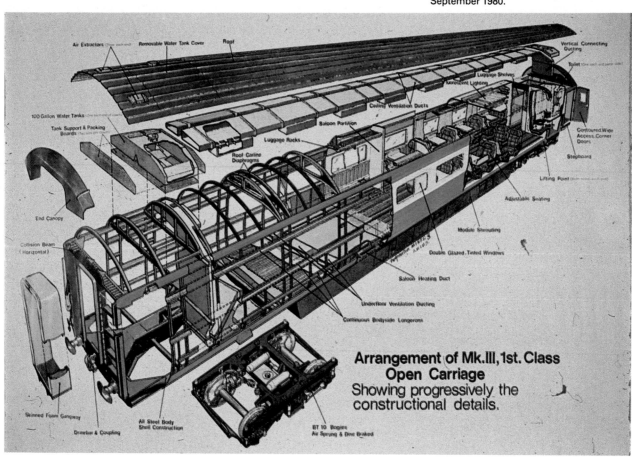

Air Extractors (One each end)
Removable Water Tank Cover
Roof
Vertical Connecting Ducting
Toilet (One each end same side)
Luggage Shelves
Fluorescent Lighting
Ceiling Ventilation Ducts
100 Gallon Water Tanks (One each end of coach)
Tank Support & Packing Boards (Two sets per end)
Saloon Partition
Luggage Racks
Contoured Wide Access Corner Doors
Roof Carline Diaphragms
Stepboard
Lifting Point (Both sides each end)
End Canopy
Adjustable Seating
Collision Beam (Horizontal)
Module Shrouding
Double Glazed Tinted Windows
Saloon Heating Duct
Underfloor Ventilation Ducting
Continuous Bodyside Longerons
Skinned Foam Gangway
All Steel Body Shell Construction
Drawbar & Coupling
BT 10 Bogies Air Sprung & Disc Braked

Arrangement of Mk.III, 1st. Class Open Carriage
Showing progressively the constructional details.

No 253.006 leaving Dainton tunnel bound for Plymouth on 7 September 1980.

Proposed Brush class 89 high speed electric locomotive for the West Coast main line.

CLASS 89

HAWKER SIDDELEY
BRUSH ELECTRICAL MACHINES LTD
TRACTION DIVISION

Inside LAIRA's maintenance depot at Plymouth.

Australian InterCity XPT as built for the New South Wales Government Railway by the Commonwealth Engineering Company.

InterCity set 253.015 approaching Dawlish Station with a northbound express from Plymouth.

HST No 252.001 near Reading in passenger service.

A Bristol up express passing the disused
Badminton Station on 31 December 1983.

InterCity 125 passing Dawlish Warren en
route from Cornwall to London.

A South Wales down express passing
Badminton on 31 December 1983.

Two InterCity 125 train sets together with a
class 50 at Paddington Station just before
midnight on 14 July 1983.

The Motive Power

Much has been said and written about the best method of propulsion for railway trains and about the relative merits of steam, electric, diesel or gas turbine power units, but in the final analysis it comes down to a combination of power requirements, weight and cost. The latter consideration also includes the types of fuel available to suit the area of operation.

The power requirement is set by the load of train to be hauled and the desired speed of operation. The main line requirements in the UK have generally resulted in a train weight of between 300 tons (304,819 kg) and 400 tons (406,425 kg), although at times, particularly during World War II, train weights of over 700 tons (711,245 kg) had to be handled. Trains of that weight used to be handled regularly every night running out of the Gare de Lyon station in Paris to various parts of Europe and, in the USA, such trains as the 'Broadway Limited' and the 'Twentieth Century' would have been usually around 1,500 tons (1,524,096 kg). These days, specialised freight trains of coal and iron ore are in the region of 20,000 tons (20,321,280 kg) or more.

The rolling resistance of a 300 ton (304,819 kg) train only requires some 480 hp to propel it on level track at 60 mph (96 km/h), but at 80 mph (129 km/h) this demand has gone up to 900 hp. At 100 mph (161 km/h) the need is for 1,600 hp and for operation at 125 mph (201 km/h) around 3,000 hp is called for, apart from wind resistance which, while quite small head on, can be quite a large sideways force. In addition, power is needed for hauling the power unit itself, whether it is in the form of a locomotive or power cars. Power is also needed in modern trains for auxiliary services such as lighting, heating and cooking.

All this adds up to a total of over 4,000 hp; while this could be provided by steam locomotives, the problem of getting the steam into and out of the cylinders at over 100 mph (161 km/h) would preclude regular operation at anything like 125 mph (201 km/h).

Electric propulsion poses no problem as far as power is concerned, but there are problems with current collection at these speeds and the lack of widespread use of electricity on the main lines of the UK.

Gas turbines can provide a lot of power in a compact and light-weight unit, but they suffer from high initial cost and a sharp fall-off in efficiency at outputs below around 80 per cent of full power. This was discovered in the trials of the two gas turbine locomotives carried out on the Western Region between 1950 and 1960; it was found that they used nearly as much oil per mile as a steam locomotive used in coal. There was also a dearth of suitable gas turbine units at approximately the power required.

This left the diesel engine as the most promising source of power. Developments in diesel engine design at that time meant that a single medium speed (1,000 rpm) engine could produce 4,000 hp, or that output could be attained by the use of two high speed (1,500 rpm) engines. Both of these engine types were of the size and weight that could be accommodated in British Rail vehicles, but the larger medium speed engine could only be accommodated in a locomotive while the high speed version could be built into a railcar.

The one 4,000 hp locomotive produced by the Brush Electrical Engineering Company in 1968

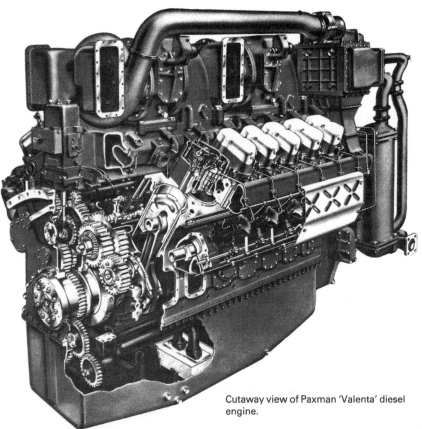

Cutaway view of Paxman 'Valenta' diesel engine.

called 'Kestrel' was designed for operation at up to 125 mph (201 km/h), but the axle load was over 21 tons (21,337 kg) and the Civil Engineer accordingly ruled out normal operation at more than 105 mph (170km/h).

Designs were then prepared for both locomotive and railcar units to embody the high speed diesel engine, but experiences with twin-engined locomotives had been far from satisfactory. The result was that the designs were rationalised into power cars using the high speed engine, and locomotives for freight duty only using the medium speed engine which has now become the class 56.

Before the design of the High Speed Train was even started, work had been proceeding with the Advanced Passenger Train, which had an even more rigorous weight limitation in view of its intended speed of 155 mph (250 km/h) and in which the axle load was limited to 16 tons (16,257 kg). The power unit adopted for this experimental Advanced Passenger Train (APT-E) was the Leyland 350 automotive gas turbine. By using four of these for propulsion in each power car an output for traction purposes of 2,400 hp was applied to a four coach train weighing only 145 tonnes (145,000 kg). There was another similar gas turbine in each power car for auxiliaries, but that did not help the traction load. That train was built purely to test the tilting and braking systems before finalising the design of a production train for commercial use.

One of the problems with higher-speed travel is the ability to stop within a given distance from maximum speed, and none of the conventional means were suitable for the use of these intended speeds on the existing rail network. The conventional means of train braking consist first of brake blocks (steel or fibre) on the wheel rim, secondly of disc brakes by pads to discs on the wheel or to a separate disc on the axle, thirdly

by regenerative braking or feeding back into the electrical supply and fourthly by rheostatic braking. The latter involves the use of the traction motors as generators which dissipate the train energy to rheostats or resistances in the form of heat, but this system involves the use of a prime mover to provide current to energise the motor fields and is suitable only when a diesel engine or gas turbine is installed. Whichever system is used, a lot of energy has to be dissipated and a lot of heat dispersed.

For the High Speed Train which was designed with two bogies per coach, it was estimated that there would be enough wheels to allow the use of disc brakes on all wheels in order to obtain the desired rate of retardation of 0.09 g. That was the requirement to stop the train from 125 mph (201 km/h) in under 6,660 ft (2,030 m) which was the

permitted distance for locomotive-hauled trains from 100 mph (161 km/h). The APT by contrast was designed as an articulated set with bogies between each coach so as to save weight and thus had fewer wheels. This led to the decision to use a hydrokinetic brake which is based on the system of dissipating the heat by pumping water instead of electricity. The system had been used on some of the German locomotives which employed hydraulic transmissions as opposed to electric and had proved effective. This hydrokinetic brake proved eventually to be the weakest part of the APT concept, but it was used on the trailer bogies of the experimental APT. On the power cars the rheostatic system of braking was used, but only for maximum speeds of up to 125 mph (201 km/h). While the gas turbine was acceptable for the

12-cylinder version of 'Valenta' diesel engine coupled to alternator as fitted in the InterCity 125.
Alternator end of power unit with Brush Alternator coupled to 2,250 hp 'Valenta' engine.
Brush TMH 68-46 traction motor producing 467 hp. Two of these are fitted in each bogie.

experimental version of the APT, there was no suitable unit available for the production version for which at least 6,000 hp per power car would be needed. This was beyond the capacity of any available diesel power so the only solution was to rely on electric propulsion, which would confine its operation to the West Coast main line between Euston, Manchester, Liverpool and Glasgow.

For the rest of the British Rail network therefore the diesel engined version was going to be needed urgently and the design, development and production were planned for fleet introduction by 1973.

In about 1960 Paxman Diesels Ltd of Colchester, formerly Davey Paxman and now a Management Company of G.E.C. Diesels Ltd, had started work on the development of a highly-rated 1,600 rpm diesel engine intended initially for application in high speed naval craft; that engine was envisaged as having an output of 4,000 hp from an 18-cylinder VEE version which would be a sprint rating for naval purposes only. The heaviest model of that engine that could be accommodated in a suitable railcar was the 12-cylinder type and the output from that at a rating suitable for rail traction purposes was 2,250 hp at 1,500 rpm; it was around that engine that the design of the power cars for the HST was based. It was found that this would allow a unit to be designed with an axle load of not more than 17 tons (17,273 kg) and thus suitable for operation at up to 125 mph (201 km/h).

Paxman Diesels had been producing high speed diesel engines for rail traction application since 1931 and had provided the engines for various locomotives for British Railways, including an 800 hp Bo-Bo No 10800, the 2,000 hp 'Fell' No 10100 and standard locomotive classes 15, 16 and 17. They had also supplied some versions of their 'Ventura'

type engine for use in a Western Region class 42 and in some re-engined versions of the class 21 locomotives in Scotland. The development work on Paxman's latest range, called the 'Valenta', was followed closely by BR engineers, including Mr T.C.B. Miller and Mr Walter Jowett who formerly had been with the English Electric Company and had tried to persuade that firm to produce a suitable high speed diesel engine – which they almost did.

The Paxman 'Valenta' engine design is of VEE form based on a 60° angle between the two cylinder banks and has a cylinder bore of 7.75 in (19.7 cm) with a stroke of 8.5 in (21.6 cm). It is a four stroke engine with single stage turbocharging with an aftercooler in order to keep the exhaust gas temperature to acceptable limits. It was estimated that by 1970 an output of 4 hp per square inch of piston area would be available which would give 2,263 hp from twelve cylinders. This entailed firing pressures of 2,000 lb per square inch and the crankcase, fabricated from steel castings, was designed to withstand that pressure. With a main journal diameter of 9 ins (23 cm) the high rubbing speed entailed the use of aluminium/tin main bearings. The pistons are single piece aluminium forgings with plain cast iron piston rings running in chrome-plated cylinder liners. The connecting rods are of the fork and blade type, and in order to allow the piston and connecting rod to be withdrawn through the cylinder liner, the big end bearings were limited to 5.5 ins (14 cm) giving a maximum bearing loading of 3,580 lb per square inch.

The cylinder heads are of cast iron with two inlet and two exhaust valves in each operated by push rods from a central camshaft. The maximum designed temperature for the exhaust valves is 650°C. Each cylinder has its own fuel pump mounted on the outside of the cylinder banks so making them

accessible for maintenance and changing. A water cooled exhaust manifold is fitted so as to eliminate the failures of the expansion bellows, and the failure rate on that item was thereby reduced from 20 to 1,000 hours to less than 1 per 1,000 hours on test. This in turn entailed a larger radiator in order to dissipate the extra seven per cent heat loss to the water in the exhaust manifold. This feature also reduces the fire risk which is important when one engine is at the far end of the train. Each engine is fitted with a Napier SA-084 turbocharger equipped with plain bearings fed from the engine lubricating oil system, which feature was later to lead to some problems in service. Since there were no DC windings in the main generator by which the engine could be motored for starting, two starter motors of the automotive type are fitted to each engine supplied from the 110 volt batteries under the power car.

The weight of the engine, complete with oil and water, is 17,402 lb (7,891 kg) giving a specific weight of 7.7 lb per hp. Both 12- and 16-cylinder versions were subject to prolonged testing for the benefit of British Rail and the Ministry of Defence during which the 12-cylinder version ran

The flexible drive unit from traction motor to wheels is necessitated by the motor being fully sprungborne in bogie.

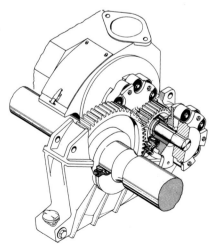

at various outputs for over 7,000 hours. Even this was not sufficient to show up some of the faults that later developed in service, which shows the magnitude of the problem for an engine manufacturer bringing a new engine into successful operation.

The Valenta diesel engine was flange mounted to a Brush alternator having twelve poles with rotating diodes on the shaft so as to produce DC for energising the rotating magnetic poles. The first design of alternator produced 1,500 volts AC for traction purposes, 110 volts DC for the engine auxiliaries and 850 volts DC for the train supply. The latter was the standard voltage at which the Mk III coaching stock was supplied from the train heating generators in conventional diesel locomotives, but this arrangement was later altered on the production HST stock.

The current for the four traction motors was rectified to DC and each traction motor was a Brush type TMH 68-46 of 467 hp permanently coupled in series-parallel. These motors were of the four pole type with class H insulation on the armature coils and class F on the field windings. The motors are fully frame-suspended in the bogie so as to reduce the unsprung weight to below 2.5 tons (2,540 kg) per axle stipulated by the Civil Engineer for operation at 125 mph (201 km/h). Since this involves more relative movement between the motor and the driving axle than with the conventional nose suspended traction motor, a special form of flexible drive is required. This is usually achieved by the use of a flexible drive pinion using springs or rubber blocks, but in this case the system adopted was to pass the drive shaft through the motor pinion and to drive that by a flexible spider. This spider consists of twelve Twinflex links round a 340 mm diameter disc which allows a relative rise and fall of 30 mm for the axle box in the bogie frame.

Disc brake and pads as fitted on InterCity 125 trains.

The gear ratio is 2.5/1 and with a 40 in (1,020 mm) diameter driving wheel the continuous motor rating at 500 amps is at 68 mph (109 km/h). The motor speed at 125 mph (201 km/h) is 2,620 rpm.

The electrical control equipment was based on the experience obtained by the Brush Electrical Engineering Company during the tests and trials of their 4,000 hp locomotive 'Kestrel' in 1968 and dates even further back to the AC transmission equipment tried out in their locomotive 'Hawk' in 1965. Basically this consists of a load regulator of the rotary transducer type, oil operated, and controlled by the engine governor. This controls the current to the alternator field through thyristor circuits, thereby adjusting the alternator output and the fuel supply to the diesel engine to meet the load demand. By means of his controller the driver selects the engine speed at which he desires to run and the load control system adjusts the engine and the alternator output accordingly.

The reversers, field diverts and heating contactors are electro-pneumatic, while all other relays are magnetically worked. The electronic control system is based on integrated units with plug-in printed circuit cards which are programmed to control the function to which they apply. Faults can quickly be remedied by the exchange of printed circuit cards or complete units.

The auxiliary generator supplies the batteries, the control circuits and the fuel and oil priming pumps, but not the cooling fan. The cooling group consists of a Voith variable speed fan driven off the free end of the engine and controlled by means of a hydrodynamic fan hub coupling. The full fan speed is 1,780 rpm and takes 155 hp to drive the 44 in (1,120 mm) diameter fan. The two aluminium radiator panels each side are designed to dissipate 1,240,000 k.cals per hour and are placed inboard of the walkway so as to provide access from the train to the engine room and the driving cab.

That completes the description of the actual power equipment in the power cars. The rest of the equipment that goes toward the making of the complete train is included in the next chapter; first in the prototype train and then in the production trains as amended by service experience during the testing of the prototype version.

The Prototype High Speed Train

By 1969 road traffic competition was causing serious losses in passenger transport, and this problem was not going to be solved in time by the Advanced Passenger Train, which was taking too long to develop. The design of an alternative High Speed Train was then embarked on. Fortunately, all the basic components were available in the form of the new Mk III coaching stock, the Paxman 'Valenta' diesel engine, and a suitable form of disc brake for the

Power cars building at Crewe works. Prototype model with the first version of the engine alternator set being lowered into position.

essential part of stopping the train from the intended speed of 125 mph (201 km/h).

When the design of the High Speed Train was initiated the selection of power units rested between diesel engines and gas turbines and an estimate was made of the total costs of these alternative forms of power supply covering the first twenty years of operation. The French trial TGV had been built using gas turbines, but it was ascertained that these needed to be overhauled every 2,000 hours. Then an aircraft gas turbine was studied, but the manufacturer would not consider any development work unless an order for 400 engines was forthcoming, but based on the available information the costs for the various types of engine worked out as follows:-

4500 HP of Power Equipment for 20 Years
Assuming 160,000 Miles per Year

	Diesel Engine	Aircraft Gas Turbine	Industrial Gas Turbine
Initial Cost	£239,000	£300,000	£280,000
Annual Maintenance	£600,000	£1,260,000	£520,000
Fuel at 5.5p/Litre	£1,925,000	£3,270,000	£2,890,000
Total	£2,764,000	£4,830,000	£3,690,000
Cost per Train Mile	8.48p	14.81p	11.32p

Completed High Speed Train at Derby prior to initial testing.
Inset: Mk III coach as finished for HST Prototype train.

This showed that the diesel engine was the correct choice of power unit for this duty. As a matter of interest the latest quoted figure for maintenance is £500,000 per annum for the complete train not just for the power unit, and of course this figure may go up as time goes on.

Since the power demand of 4,500 hp required the use of two 12-cylinder diesel engines, the choice lay between a twin-engined locomotive or the use of two power cars, one at each end of the train. The locomotive solution might have been marginally less expensive, but the use of power cars meant a quicker turnround at terminal stations since the whole trainset could be worked just like an electric train; the basis of the whole network was planned for high utilisation with minimal time for turnround. The major disadvantage was that the maintenance depots had to be planned to handle complete trains and this has posed certain problems in practice.

In August 1970 a sum of £800,000 was allocated by the BR Board for the development of the High Speed Train which was to allow for the building of two power cars and nine Mk III passenger carriages. But the initial design, carried out at Derby, was based on a seven coach set with the two power cars weighing in total around 380 tons (386,104 kg) depending on formation make-up, the intended formation being two first class cars, four second class and one kitchen or buffet car.

The construction of the power cars was carried out at the Crewe works of British Rail Engineering Ltd (BREL) as the workshop organisation of BR has been designated since 1 January 1970, while the carriages were selected from those being produced at the Litchurch Lane Carriage & Wagon works at Derby.

The assembly of the complete prototype train took place at Derby in June 1972 and consisted of the two power cars, five cars of standard Mk III stock, a Mk I buffet car and a specially equipped test coach.

Each power car was built to the same basic design as the Mk III coaching stock and was of the Bo-Bo type with an overall length of 57 ft 8 in (17.6 m) and a designed weight of 66 tons (67,060 kg). It was important to keep the unsprung weight down to the figure of 2.2 tons (2,540 kg) specified by the Civil Engineer and this was achieved as follows:

Wheels	854 kg
Axle	394 kg
Brake discs	296 kg
Axle boxes	227 kg
Bearings	50 kg
Wheelslide detectors	20 kg
Suspension links and dampers	103 kg
Gearbox and pinion	272 kg
Total	2216 kg

The diesel engine was mounted almost centrally between the two bogies with the alternator and control gear at the driver's end with a bulkhead between the engine compartment and the alternator. This kept the electrical compartment free from engine oil and fumes, and helped to reduce the noise level in the driving compartment. There was also a double thickness bulkhead between the electrical room and the driving cab. The cab was built in the form of a monocoque reinforced foam sandwich which was developed at the Plastic Development Centre at Derby. The two skins of the cab were each of a three stage laminate form spaced 2 in (50 mm) apart and this space was filled with glass-reinforced fibre. All the conduits for the control wiring as well as the brake air pipes and ventilation ducts were also in this space. The cabs were bolted to the main frame by resilient fixtures and incorporate sound proofing, heating and ventilation. The driver was seated centrally with a well laid out control panel having the power control lever to his right hand and the brake control to his left. The two main indicators showed speed in mph and brake pipe pressure in lb/sq in.

In front of the driver the windscreen was of high-impact safety glass 4 ft (1.2 m) by 2 ft 6 ins (0.8 m) and 1 in (25 mm) thick designed to withstand the impact of a 2 lb (0.9 kg) weight at 190 mph (306 km/h). Apart from objects thrown up from the track, vandals have caused drivers' deaths by throwing objects from bridges; and large birds can be quite a hazard, especially at night. Accommodation was also provided for an assistant in a tip-up seat on the bulkhead behind the driver, but this did not prove satisfactory and was only used on the prototype build.

The driver's power controller covered both power cars and used the Westcode digital system suitable for single wire control. The driver's controller selected engine speed and the individual engine control system selected the excitation and fuel rack position suitable to that particular engine, automatically adjusting the engine output to suit the engine condition. In the event of a flashover of a traction motor, protection from short circuit was provided by a contactor on the top of each control cubicle. The power control panel also embodied engine starting and stopping as well as a selector for forward or reverse running.

The brake controls were by the Westinghouse Company's Westcode system DW-1 in one power car and by the Davies & Metcalfe E.70 system in the other. The main disc brakes were by Girling and the discs were bolted on either side of the wheel webs. On the power cars only, cast iron scrubber blocks were provided on each wheel to prevent the tyres becoming too smooth and these blocks were used for the parking brake.

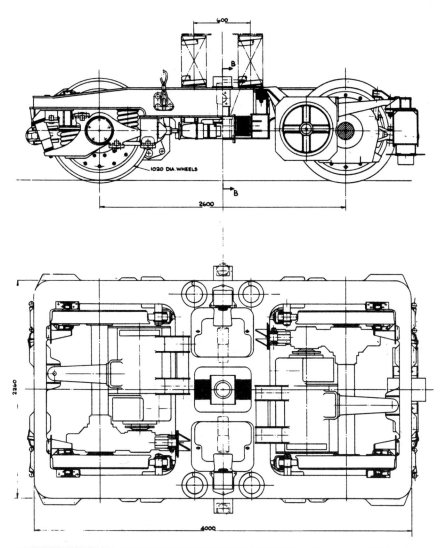

600

B

1020 DIA WHEELS

2600

B

2260

4000

From the driver's cab a single door led to the electrical compartment from where two doors, one each side, led past the engine and the radiators. After the intense noise of the engine room a door through another double bulkhead led to the comparative peace of a luggage space in which an enclosed guard's compartment housed the controls for an auxiliary driving position. Consideration had been given to placing some passenger seats in the space in the power car not filled with equipment; but this possibility was ruled out after the disastrous experience of the Blue Pullmans, in which the power car ride for the passengers was extremely unpleasant.

Under the power car were located a spillage tank for any fuel, oil or water that leaked into the engine room, the main fuel tanks having a capacity of 1,250 gallons (5,500 litres), sufficient for 1,000 miles (1,609 km) of operation and the batteries for engine starting and controls. Each power car also had a Davies & Metcalfe air compressor of the two stage type 2A115 for the brakes and this was driven by a 110 volt DC motor.

The power car roof which had translucent panels over the engine and the electrical equipment, was arranged to lift off in sections so that the complete power unit, the control cubicle or the cooler group could be lifted out for exchange or maintenance.

The power car was mounted on two bogies of the BP.5 type. This was a variation of the B.4 bogie first used under the Mk II coaches in 1956 and used coil suspension and long swing links with vertical, lateral and rotational damping by Koni shock absorbers. The axleboxes were mounted in a radial arm and the 40 in (102 cm) wheels were shrunk onto a hollow

Layout of BP.5 bogie showing traction motors and flexicoil mounting springs. *Below:* DOC II bogie as used for passenger cars in the HST prototype train.

The High Speed Train passing Durham
during early testing days.

axle. The bogie was redesigned to
accommodate two traction motors
and the car body rested on four
flexicoil springs per bogie, each
carrying a load of 5.5 tons
(5,588 kg). These bogies were of
welded construction and were a
development of those fitted to the
class 86 electric locomotive

number E.3173 on which the
flexicoil system was tried out; that
particular locomotive was
regeared to run at up to 125 mph
(201 km/h) for trials on this
suspension system.

The Mk III passenger vehicles
making up the rest of the train
were as previously described
except that they were equipped
with a DOC II bogie. These cars
were all fitted in the prototype
version with a motor alternator

designed to produce alternating
current for the fluorescent lighting
and running off the 850 DC supply
which was the standard system
supplied by diesel locomotives
equipped with electric train
heating (ETH).

The power cars and the train
layout were all designed at Derby
and, with the co-operation of the
firms supplying all the equipment,
the first two power cars were
wheeled in April 1972, and the

whole set was ready for test running in June of that year. The whole project then ran into a major problem that had not been foreseen: the train drivers' union (ASLEF) wanted more money for working these trains at the higher speeds proposed.

Perhaps this should have been anticipated, but once these disputes begin they take a lot of time to sort out and it was over a year before trial running could take place at over 100 mph (161 km/h). The initial operation took place mostly between Kings Cross and Darlington; but although acceleration rates could be tested, the crucial braking trials could not be carried out. Agreement was finally reached over the operating, by June 1973, and on 12 June a speed of 143 mph (230 km/h) was achieved on the racing stretch of track between Thirsk and Tollerton.

The braking tests showed that the train could be stopped from 125 mph (201 km/h) in 5,790 ft (1,765 m) and during these trials, as if to test the windscreen, a large piece of ballast hit the screen at 130 mph (209 km/h) which resulted in just grazing the outer skin. There was evidence of bogie hunting at 129 mph (207 km/h), and although this was above the intended rates of normal travel, the lateral dampers were strengthened to counter this problem in case it showed up later at lower speeds.

There were problems with water getting into the traction motors and, because the fans in these motors were very noisy, separate blowers for the cooling air for these motors were fitted in the production trains. The smell of the disc brakes found its way into the passenger cars via the air conditioning intake so it was arranged for the inlet ducts to be closed during heavy braking. This trouble is still not completely solved since air finds its way in through the gangways and the outer doors.

It had been intended initially to uprate the diesel engine to 2,500 hp so as to allow for the operation of an extra coach for service on the East Coast main line and after some running a modified turbocharger was fitted, but the results showed unduly high engine temperatures and the rating was restored to the original output of 2,250 hp, at which figure it still remains.

It was also found during running at 125 mph (201 km/h) that it was necessary for the second man in the cab to look out for and warn any maintenance staff in the way of the train, thus making it desirable for both crew members to sit side by side. The cab arrangement was modified accordingly for the production trains to incorporate this feature and side windows were added to improve visibility.

Some other features showed up during the testing of this prototype train that resulted in modifications to the design and these will be included in the description of the production version.

The prototype power cars were classed as locomotive type 41 which had originally been intended for the five North British A1A-A1A 2,000 hp diesel hydraulics Nos D.600/604, but they were withdrawn before the present classification system could be applied. The prototype train was later classed as 252.001 and as such entered public service on the Western Region on 5 May 1975 working the 10.15 from Paddington to Bath, Bristol and Weston-Super-Mare.

On 2 August 1973 a special demonstration run was made from Kings Cross to Darlington and back. The guests of the Chairman of British Railways Board, the Rt. Hon. Richard Marsh, included Mr Keith Speed of the Department of the Environment, other Members of Parliament, Trade Union officials and the gentlemen of the press.

As far as York the speed was limited to 100 mph (161 km/h) so as to fit into the existing Deltic timetable and the 188 miles (303 km) to York took 141 minutes. After York and on the racing ground of the former North Eastern Railway 252.001 was let go and from reaching 122 mph (196 km/h) at 11 miles (18 km) from York, the next 15 miles (24 km) were run in 7 minutes 3 seconds at an average of 127.6 mph (204 km/h). An emergency brake stop was then made which showed that the train could be stopped from that speed in 58 seconds in a distance of 2,020 yards (1,853 m), well within the permitted figure of 2,250 yards (2,060 m).

On the return journey the 44.1 miles (71 km) from Darlington to York were run without any brake tests in 27 minutes 37 seconds (95.8 mph/154 km/h) and the 188.2 miles (302.5 km) from York to London were run in 137 minutes 23 seconds with a brief maximum of 102 mph (164 km/h) near Peterborough. This run showed that a two hour timing could be achieved from London to York and this is now being worked to in the current timetables.

Prior to its entry into public service the prototype train had run some 120,000 miles and it continued throughout the summer of 1975 with two round trips a day working at a maximum of 100 mph (161 km/h) so as to fit into the existing timetable. One of its last functions had been to act as a special train conveying the Duke of Edinburgh from York to Eaglescliffe in September 1975 when he inaugurated the 'Rail 150 Pageant' in Preston Park, Stockton.

It was withdrawn in November that year and the two power cars were modified to act as control units for the power cars of the Advanced Passenger Train when these were tested on the London Midland Region electrified line in 1979. The prototype train was then sent to the National Railway Museum at York having completed just over 200,000 miles of operation.

The Production Version Classes 253 & 254

The 95 sets of InterCity 125 High Speed Trains were provided for British Rail by BREL (British Rail Engineering Ltd) between 1976 and 1982, the first complete allocation being 27 sets of 253 stock to the Western Region delivered by May 1977.

The 253 trains comprised seven passenger cars and two power cars generally similar to the Prototype HST described in the previous chapter, but as a result of the development testing of the prototype train certain improvements were incorporated in the production versions.

As previously mentioned, the design of the driver's cab was altered to allow for the two occupants to sit side by side. This allowed the relief driver to be ready to operate the warning horn immediately any staff were noted in the path of the train since at the rate of 61 yards per second there is not much time to clear the track. Full air conditioning was also provided as well as better sound proofing and the ride in the cab is excellent. The engine noise is barely noticeable except when the door to the electrical compartment is opened. Windscreens are prone to leakage in the rain, as they are with other locomotives.

The rest of the power car was similar to the original version except that the radiator was moved nearer the engine thus allowing nearly one foot of extra room in the luggage compartment. In the original layout enough room had been left for a 16-cylinder engine in case this was found to be desirable, but the extra weight could not be accepted on account of the axle load limitation, and as a result the radiator could be moved towards the engine. The radiator

cooling capacity was also increased from 1,234,000 kcals/h (kilocalories per hour) to 1,436,000 kcals/h to allow for higher fuel consumption than originally estimated and for a higher compressor outlet temperature from the turbocharger.

A modified load regulator based on a three phase Thyristor bridge circuit replaced the original DC chopper type and the auxiliary train supply was completely redesigned. Since the trains were to be of fixed formation, the coaches would not be called on to work in locomotive-hauled inter-city trains, and it was decided that the supply for all the coaches and the engine auxiliaries would be at 415 volts 3 phase 50 Hz, thus eliminating the 850 volt train supply and the motor alternators in each coach. Though this output would be down to as low as 270 volts 33 Hz at minimum engine speed this was overcome in the case of the micro-aire ovens in the catering vehicles by supplying these through a transformer with primary tap changing. It was estimated that the adoption of this system could save around £3 million over the whole programme for a twenty year life. This auxiliary supply can be fed from either power unit and avoids the problem of synchronization.

The traction motors were redesigned for forced air ventilation because water tended to get into them, and this resulted in a considerable reduction in noise level. The controls in the guard's compartment were eliminated since movements of an isolated power car would be very infrequent.

The passenger coaches were generally similar to the Mk III stock

in the prototype train, but since these were to be in fixed formation the buffers were eliminated and buck-eye couplings adopted throughout. The electrical system was also altered to take the 415 volt 3 phase 50 Hz supply and an improved method of sealing the air intake during braking was adopted, in an attempt to try to avoid the smell of hot brake pads, but there are still complaints about this feature. Consideration was given to the use of chemical toilets and though these are used in the APT they were not adopted for the InterCity 125 sets.

The first production train sets were introduced into service in the Western Region in October 1976 starting with set 253.001. These had been planned to start a year earlier, but the twelve month delay in testing the prototype train due to 'industrial inaction' resulted in the production trains being late to enable any faults found in the prototype to be eliminated before the production line was started.

Initially the first sets operated from London (Paddington) to South Wales and to Weston-Super-Mare thus providing high speed services to Reading, Swindon, Chippenham, Bath, Bristol, Newport, Cardiff and Swansea.

Maintenance depots were established at London (Old Oak Common) and at Bristol (St Philips Marsh) with fuelling facilities at Cardiff and at Swansea. Each depot has a covered shed with three roads having centre and side pits. There is an external fuelling road and a further road for a mechanical coach washing machine. Each covered road takes a complete train with room for uncoupling to examine the couplers and the middle road has two 1.5 tonne (1,500 kg) overhead gantries. Fork-lift trucks capable of handling 2.5 tonnes (2,500 kg) are used to change the under floor modules on the coaches and power cars while four power jacks enable bogies to be changed. It was a pity that the lifting facilities did not permit the lifting out of power units since the power cars have to be moved to the nearest locomotive depot for this to be carried out. The depot at St Philips Marsh has through running roads, but at Old Oak Common the mainshed had to be arranged with dead end roads due to the limitation of space. This makes the operation of removing a power car to the locomotive maintenance shed a difficult and time-consuming exercise if use needs to be made of the 50 ton (50,803 kg) overhead crane in that shed. It also involves the use of a signalled path since part of the route is beyond depot limits.

By May 1977 the planned 27 sets had been delivered to the Western Region and a revised and faster timetable was instigated. The fastest train in 1976 was the 16.29 from Reading to Bristol (Parkway) a distance of 75.8 miles (122 km) at 95.7 mph (153 km/h). Parkway was a special commuter station to the north of Bristol on the South Wales line with special car parking facilities for 1,000 cars and with easy access to the M4 and M5 motorways. In the revised Western Region timetable there were initially eleven trains a day at start to stop average speeds of over 90 mph (145 km/h) and 48 at over 80 mph (129 km/h), a cumulative daily mileage of 3,647 miles (5,870 km).

With the ability to reach 100 mph (161 km/h) in under four miles and 125 mph (201 km/h) in under ten miles (16 km) on the level from a standing start, it was not long before trains were being timed at over 100 mph (161 km/h) from start to stop and this was a tonic to the Western and a return to the old days of the 'Cheltenham Flyer' when they led the world in operating speeds.

By May 1977 the revised timetable did call for some runs at an average start to stop speed of over 100 mph (161 km/h) and on 7

HST, now numbered 252.001, at Swindon in passenger service alongside APT.E. which has completed its testing.

May a couple of Jubilee Special runs covered the 117.6 miles (189 km) from Bristol to Paddington in 68 minutes 23 seconds one way and 67 minutes 35 seconds the other. The average speeds were 103.3 mph (165.3 km/h) and 104.4 mph (167 km/h). The drivers for this joint effort were W.H. Francis and R.J. Sandercock for the up run and A. Williams and W.J.V. Jones for the down journey. It is interesting to compare these two runs of over one hundred miles (161 km) in both directions with the solitary downhill dash of the LNER *Mallard* in 1938 when it just reached 126 mph (203 km/h) momentarily; on the occasion of the record runs on 7 May whole stretches of track were being run at 125 mph (201 km/h) in both directions. The InterCity 125 trains incidentally had about three times the power output of *Mallard* (see page 55 for details).

The second batch of 32 InterCity 125 trains were allocated to the Eastern and Scottish Regions to work the East Coast main line between London (Kings Cross) and Edinburgh and then continuing on over the Forth and Tay bridges to Aberdeen.

This was the route over which the East Coast contenders for the 'Race to the North' of 1895 comprising the former Great Northern, North Eastern and North British Railways had run the 523 miles (842 km) from Kings Cross to Aberdeen in 520 minutes; only to be beaten by the West Coast combination of the London and North Western and the Caledonian Railways who ran their route of 540 miles (869 km) in 512 minutes.

In that contest the West Coast companies gained through only having to make three stops at Crewe, Carlisle and Perth. In this they made better use of their system of water pick up troughs and their longest non-stop run was the 158 miles (254 km) from Euston to Crewe, covered at 64 mph (103 km/h).

On the East Coast route the longest run and the fastest was the 125 miles (201 km) from Newcastle to Edinburgh covered in 114 minutes at 66 mph (106 km/h). Not all the speed limits were observed as they should have been and the few genuine passengers got a ride they were not likely to forget.

Section view of power car for class 253 HST.

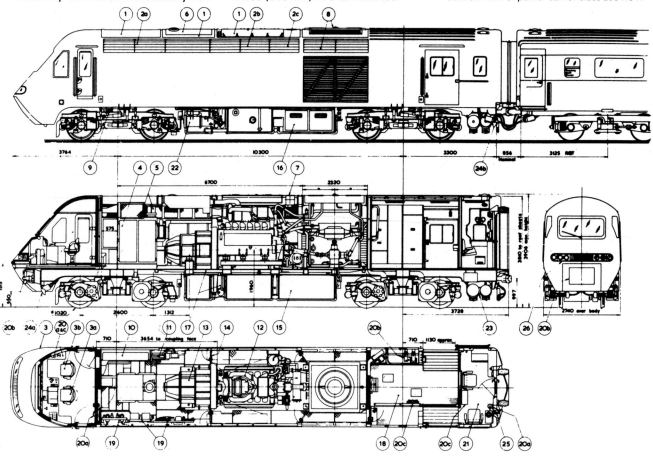

1. Translucent Roof Panels
2. Filtered Air Intakes for:—
  a Electric m/cs & clean air compartment
  b Engine combustion
  c Engine Room ventilation
3. Driving Cab with:
  a Driving position
  b Assistant's Seat
4. Electric Control Cubicle
5. Resistance Unit & Short Circuiter
6. Silencer
7. Engine Room Fan
8. Cooling Unit
9. Flexicoil Suspension
10. Rectifier Unit
11. Battery Charging Unit
12. Paxman 'Valenta' Engine, 12 RP 200L
13. Alternators
14. Clean Air Compartment Partition
15. Fuel Tank, 5 680 litre max^m
16. Battery Box
17. Spillage Tray & Collecting Tank
18. Luggage Van 1 tonne Nominal
19. Brake & other Pneumatic Equipment
20. Emergency & Safety Equipment:—
  a Fire Extinguishers
  b Towing & Propelling
20. c First Aid & Safety
21. Guard's Compartment
22. Air Compressor
23. Main Reservoirs
24. Train Electric Supplies 415V, 3 phase:—
  a Shore supply
  b Between cars
25. Parking Brake
26. Horns & Lights

**B.R. class 253
POWER CAR FOR
HIGH SPEED TRAIN**

Aided by the Gresley 'Pacifics' and later by the 'Deltics', the East Coast route regained the supremacy in speed over its rival and the InterCity 125 trains secured it. However, the East Coast will shortly be challenged by the West Coast route, when the proposed new high speed electric motive power gets into service.

By 1973 most of the track on the East Coast route had been upgraded to 105 mph (169 km/h) for the final speed-up of the Deltic services, but further improvements were needed for the HST services with their 125 mph (201 km/h) levels of operation; this process was not quite completed when the

Cutaway view of power car for production InterCity 125 trains.

1978 timetable came into force. There were some seven restrictions to 20 mph (32 km/h) for track realignment but by 1982 the route was cleared for working at 125 mph (201 km/h) most of the way to Newcastle.

The virtual rebuilding of the East Coast main line involved an expenditure of about £100 million in track and signalling equipment. The entire route was controlled from only six signal boxes at Kings Cross, Peterborough, Doncaster, York, Newcastle and Edinburgh. The last semaphore signal was removed from Doncaster on 27 September 1978. Realignment at Peterborough has permitted the speed to be raised from 20 mph (32 km/h) to 105 mph (169 km/h), but special measures have to be taken across the fens in that area

owing to continuous shrinkage of the soil. The first railbed was on a raft of faggots and a post sunk into the peat in 1851 is now fourteen feet out of the ground. The right angle crossing near Retford was eliminated and 181 farm occupation crossings had to be closed.

Continuous welded rail (CWR) is used throughout with butt welds at sixty feet (18 m) intervals and site welds at 300-1,200 feet (91-366 m) intervals. The rails are adjusted to eliminate stress at 80°F and temperatures of up to 125°F (52°C) can be accommodated in summer. Inspection for flaws is carried out using ultrasonic methods by a special test train backed up by the usual permanent way maintenance gangs.

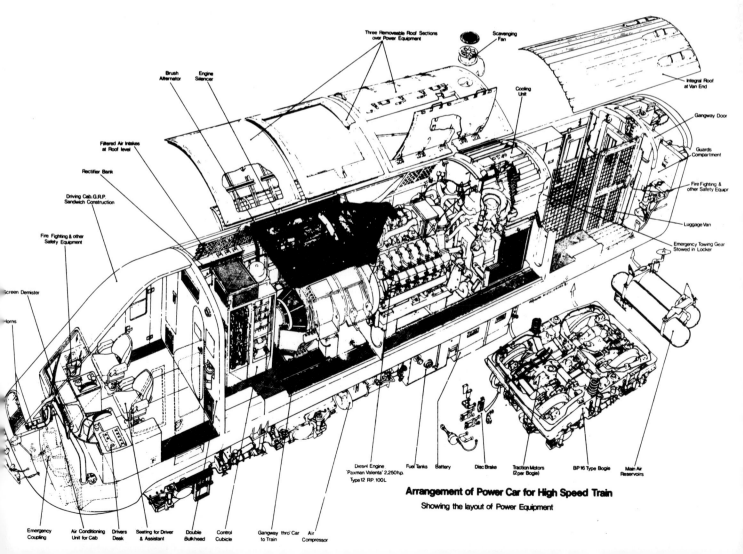

Arrangement of Power Car for High Speed Train

Showing the layout of Power Equipment

Production model power cars for 253 trains being built at Crewe works.

As a result of the Great Northern electrification scheme opened in 1978, most of the suburban traffic previously handled at Kings Cross was routed to Moorgate, which enabled the layout at Kings Cross to be simplified. One bore out of three in each of the Gas Works and Copenhagen tunnels was eliminated with two-way working in each of the remaining bores, and the platforms were reduced from seventeen to ten, which helped to speed up entry and exit times for the HST service.

There were still speed restrictions of 60 mph (96.5 km/h) at Selby for the swing bridge, 35 mph (56 km/h) at York with its sharp curve and 75 mph (121 km/h) at Durham, but most trains are arranged to stop at York or Durham or both. The 1982 timings that resulted from the improved track were 188 minutes to Newcastle (91 mph/146 km/h) compared with 258 minutes for the 1895 run; 275 minutes to Edinburgh (85.7 mph/138 km/h) compared with 375 minutes in 1895 and to Aberdeen the best time was 437 minutes (71.8 mph/116 km/h) compared with the 520 minutes of the lightweight flyer of 1895. These are not just one-off runs, they are run several times a day in both directions. Not only that but in 1979 there were two trains a day running at start to stop speeds of 106.5 mph (171 km/h) between Stevenage and Peterborough and six a day at over 100 mph

(161 km/h) between Kings Cross and Peterborough. The weekly distance run at over 90 mph (145 km/h) was 7,652 miles (12,314 km) on the East Coast and 4,984 miles (8,021 km) on the Western Region, making a total of 12,636 miles (20,335 km) compared with 5,182 miles (8,340 km) in 1978.

These speeds could not be achieved without careful preparation and maintenance of the track which involved first the detection of any faults in the track levels and then their rectification. The fault detection is done by means of specially equipped vehicles and the faults are corrected by mechanised tamping machinery provided by Plasser und Theurer. These machines were first introduced in Austria in 1953 and are now widely used in the UK and throughout the European rail network.

For the East Coast route the InterCity 125 consisted of an extra second class car making it a 2 + 8 formation carrying the category 254 and the 32 sets were distributed to depots as follows: Leeds (Neville Hill) 17 sets; Edinburgh (Craigentinny) five sets; Newcastle (Heaton) five sets and London (Bounds Green) five sets. There were 25 operating diagrams (implying 78 per cent availability) with six sets stabled at Edinburgh, four at Newcastle, seven at Leeds and eight at London.

These depots are generally similar to those on the Western Region, but the one at Bounds Green consists of a six road

extension to the existing car repair shop. At Heaton a new shed with seven tracks was installed, part of which is used for servicing diesel multiple units in the Newcastle area. The Neville Hill depot comprises a two road maintenance, shed and here a 20 tonne (20,000 kg) crane is provided which can lift out power units if necessary.

The daily servicing involves external and internal cleaning, checking and filling water and fuel tanks and checking report books for defects. Every two days an 'A' examination covers any components likely to involve safety in operation as well as checks in oil levels and taking samples of engine oil. The other examinations are at monthly 'B', three monthly 'C' and six monthly 'D' intervals with an annual visit to BREL main works at Derby for overhaul and refurbishing, by which time the set will have run between 250,000-350,000 miles (402,325-563,255 km) dependent on diagrams operated.

It was most unfortunate that the tunnel at Penmanshiel, between Newcastle and Edinburgh, collapsed just before the introduction of the HST service on the East Coast route, since that collapse meant that the 'Flying Scotsman' had to terminate at Newcastle until the newly-routed Penmanshiel line was built to by-pass the tunnel.

On 10 April 1979 the Western Region main line from Paddington to Chippenham was completely free of any speed restrictions due to maintenance work and the only speed limits in force were the usual 80 mph (129 km/h) at Reading and the 100 mph (161 km/h) one through Swindon. Accordingly the 09.20 left Platform seven at Paddington and proceeded to run the 94 miles (151 km) to Chippenham in 50 minutes 32 seconds at an average speed of 111.6 mph (179 km/h). As log 3 (p. 55) shows, once 100 mph (161 km/h) had been attained just past Ealing Broadway the speed only fell below that at Reading and at Swindon. The average from Southall to one mile short of Chippenham was 120.2 mph (193 km/h) with nowhere higher than 126.3 mph (203 km/h). These trains are very sensitive to the controls and it is only too easy to exceed the 125 mph (201 km/h) mark on good level track. Just to show that this was no mere fluke, on 27 April the 17.20 from Paddington ran the 58 miles (93 km) from Reading to Chippenham in 31 minutes 10 seconds at an average of 111.7 mph (180 km/h).

At that time both these runs were 5 mph (8 km/h) better than the then world's fastest run from Tokyo to Nagoya on the Shinkansen line in Japan, where the best recorded time was 120 minutes for the 213.5 miles (343 km) at 106.7 mph (172 km/h). Since then of course the new Paris-Lyon line of the SNCF have improved on this with their 120 minutes run for the 265.3 miles (426 km) from Paris to Lyon Part Dieu at 132.7 mph (214 km/h), but both of these are with electric traction on completely new purpose-built railway systems.

In August 1979 the Western Region were allocated fourteen more sets with the 2 + 7 formation to inaugurate services to the West of England and for this operation maintenance facilities were provided at Plymouth (Laira) with overnight stabling and fuelling facilities at Penzance.

There are two named HST trains now running between Paddington and Penzance which cover the 305 miles (491 km) to Penzance in 295 minutes with stops at Reading, Exeter, Plymouth, Liskeard, Bodmin Road, Par, St Austell, Truro, Redruth and St Erth. These two trains are the 'Cornish Riviera' and the 'Golden Hind'.

Let us take a trip in an InterCity 125 on this famous piece of line in the latest 'Cornish Riviera', seeing it from the sharp end in the driver's cab. The Riviera leaves Paddington at 09.45, the stock having already

done a run up from Swansea and getting a quick clean at Paddington. The driver's cab is warm, comfortable and clean, very different from the footplate of the steam locomotive and no drivers now want to see them back in service. Leaving Paddington we are up to 100 mph (161 km/h) by Ealing Broadway (5.6 miles/9 km) and reach the 125 mph (201 km/h) mark by Hayes (10.8 miles/17 km).

Just before Maidenhead we cross the River Thames on Brunel's famous long arch brick bridge which the experts said would fall down, but it is still giving yeoman service. A gentle climb at 1 in 1300 brings us through Sonning cutting to Reading where we stop after 22 minutes for the 36 miles (58 km).

From Reading we turn left off Brunel's main line to follow the valley of the River Kennett along which the Kennett and Avon canal once took travellers from London to Bristol. This is a very different stretch of line from the first 36 miles and winds alongside the river, climbing steadily all the way to Savernake Forest. We pass Aldermaston where once water was picked up from the troughs, through Newbury and Hungerford. Most of this stretch is limited to 90 mph (145 km/h), but short pieces

have been uprated to 100 mph (161 km/h) and it takes skilful driving to keep to the maximum allowed without having to apply the brakes too hard. The drivers know how the smell of brakes can permeate into the passenger saloons and try to keep braking to a minimum.

The grades on this line do not make much impression on the InterCity 125 which maintains a steady 80/90 mph (129/145 km/h) uphill and downhill except for speed limits which are fairly frequent on this length of line.

When a visitor is allowed a ride in the cab an Inspector always travels as well and the cab becomes crowded. The relief driver usually gives up his seat, provided his look-out duty is properly taken care of, but over the last twenty miles an opportunity is taken to walk through the train with the Inspector to check the power unit at the tail end. This gives an opportunity to make use of the toilet and refreshment facilities on the train and to test the ride in all the coaching stock. One BR engineer remarked that it is advisable to take a screwdriver along since the toilet doors have been known to get stuck and the only solution is for the trapped occupant to remove the door from

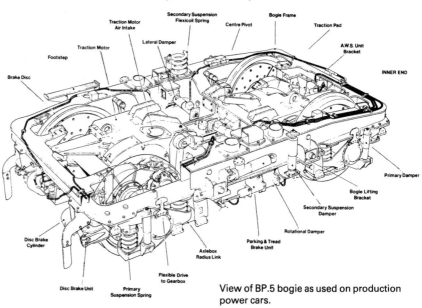

View of BP.5 bogie as used on production power cars.

Buffet car in InterCity 125 livery.

its hinges. Passing through the engine compartment when on full power is quite traumatic and really calls for ear plugs since the sound level is well above 110 decibels. The heat in the engine room is in sharp contrast to the draught of cool air when passing the radiator section.

We arrive back in the cab at Taunton in time to see the first of the three major ascents which, though nothing compared to those 1,000 feet climbs over Shap and Beattock on the West Coast main line, were quite a problem for a steam locomotive after 150 miles (241 km) of hard going. From Taunton the next eleven miles (17.7 km) gradually steepen from 1 in 174 to a final of 1 in 80 to the summit at Whiteball Tunnel. It was down this stretch of line that the *City of Truro* hauling the Ocean Mail was reputed to have reached 104 mph (167 km/h) in 1904. Though doubts have been cast about the actual maximum, it was certainly not far off the 100 mph (161 km/h) mark and it meant that the steam locomotive was the fastest thing in the world, since it was not until later that year that the first automobile was officially timed at over 100 mph (161 km/h) near Ostend.

The steam-hauled 'Riviera' would have been brought down to around 40 mph (64 km/h) by Whiteball while the diesel-hauled version would have come down to 65 mph (105 km/h), but the HST does not drop below 86 mph (138 km/h) with the application of full power for the final five miles (8 km) of the climb. Once through Whiteball Tunnel the speed soon goes up to 95 mph (153 km/h), but there are still some speed

restrictions to 75 mph (121 km/h) and 80 mph (129 km/h) to be negotiated before we stop at Exeter in 100 minutes for the 137.5 miles (221 km) from Reading (82.5 mph/133 km/h). On this last downhill twenty miles (32 km) from Whiteball to Exeter the diesel-hauled 'Riviera' would also have been running at up to 90 mph (145 km/h) while the steam-hauled version could have notched up another 80 mph (129 km/h).

The steam-hauled train, now down to 380 tons (386,104 kg) after dropping its slip portions at Westbury and Taunton, would have shed a further three coaches for Exeter which it would have cleared in 174 minutes from Paddington, an average of almost 60 mph (96 km/h); the 330 ton (335,301 kg) diesel loco-hauled version was timed to stop at Exeter in 139 minutes (75 mph/121 km/h) while our HST has completed this position, including a stop at Reading, in 123 minutes (84.7 mph/136 km/h). (See logs 4-6, pp. 55/56.)

At Exeter the driving crews are changed and we set out on the most picturesque section of the route along the course of the River Exe and beside the sea at Starcross and Dawlish Warren, probably one of the most photogenic pieces of railway line in the world. After dodging in and out of the four short tunnels, we turn inland at Teignmouth and after Newton Abbot where we have to come down to 40 mph (64 km/h), we come on the sudden sharp ascent to Dainton, only three miles (5 km), but at adverse grades of 1 in 40 which used to bring a 'King' and a 'Castle' down to 25 mph (40 km/h). The InterCity 125, however, accelerates up this to top the

summit at 50 mph (80.5 km/h), though the driver has to keep a careful watch on the ammeter to ensure that the traction meters are not overheated. The equally sharp descent to Totnes does not allow more than 60 mph (96.5 km/h) and then we are on the last and final stiff piece of climbing to Wrangaton, ten miles (16 km) at grades up to 1 in 40 which would have again brought the steam locomotive down to 30 mph (48 km/h). Again our HST holds its speed steady at 60 mph (96.5 km/h) until we have to slow for a speed restriction of 45 mph (72 km/h) at Tigley Box, but by the summit we are up to 65 mph (105 km/h) again.

The final length from Wrangaton to Plymouth is down the 1 in 42 of Hemerdon Bank and it was on this grade that the Gas Turbine locomotive, No 18000, burned out one of its traction motors while trying to start a train heavier than it was designed to do. This Region lays great store on keeping traction motor loads below their indicated limits and so far there has been no trouble on these short but stiff climbs.

We cover the 52 miles (84 km) from Exeter in just 53 minutes compared to the 66 minutes taken by the steam-hauled version, but only by the merit of better uphill speeds since our one maximum at 90 mph (145 km/h) was only of very short duration. We arrive at Plymouth just three hours after leaving Paddington compared to the four hours of eighty years ago.

After Plymouth the winding and hilly nature of the route precludes any speeds much higher than 60 mph (96.5 km/h) and with seven intermediate stops it takes 98 minutes running time to cover the 82.8 miles (133 km) to Penzance. The 'Riviera' becomes almost a commuter train with none of the stages longer than the 17.8 miles (29 km) from Plymouth to Liskeard. This seems an expensive waste, but without this section the train would not be worthy of the name 'Cornish Riviera Express'.

Problems in Service

On British Railways the figure for reliability is quoted in terms of kilometre per failure, a failure being a technical defect which delays a train for more than five minutes after its alloted arrival time. This is far more onerous than most countries which adopt a delay time of one hour as the figure which denotes a failure. This does not mean that every time a train is five or more minutes late that it has suffered a defect since delays can be due to many other reasons. These include other trains running late, permanent way works or signalling problems, though some recovery time is allowed in every timetable to take account of these eventualities.

For the InterCity 125 the failure rate is currently around 20,000 km per casualty; fortunately there are very few complete train failures because of having two power cars.

The first of the batch of production 253 class HST sets had just gone into service on the Western Region in 1976 when there was a full scale alert over the Mk III passenger car BT.10 bogies. A fractured axlebox housing had been discovered on a locomotive-hauled coach near Derby and an immediate inspection was undertaken on all the HST stock, which disclosed some incipient cracks in that component. A modified design of housing was quickly produced and these were rushed to Old Oak Common and to St Philips Marsh for fitting to any suspect coaches.

To avoid breaking up train sets two spare bogies were prepared with the new axlebox housings and, as soon as any coach showed signs of a crack in that component, both bogies were changed. The bogies removed were then refitted with the new housings ready for the next defective coach to show up.

Just as the bogie problem was being surmounted some problems began to show up in the power units. These had not showed up in the prototype train (252.001), probably because it had not been worked nearly as hard as the new batch of 253 class production trains with their much more intensive timetable.

The first of these problems was fractures in the cylinder heads of the diesel engine, which were caused partly by the use of an incorrect material and by the casting methods adopted; once the cause was known this problem was soon solved. The real trouble that arose as a result of these defects was that water found its way into the lubricating oil and the anti-freeze in the water attacked the material of the thrust bearings in the turbocharger. This was particularly unfortunate because for a long time diesel engine builders had been trying to get the turbocharger manufacturers to produce a machine that would work off the engine oil system. To obviate this attack, oil samples

253.010 InterCity 125 set in Sonning Cutting on the Western Region of BR, showing exhaust fouling of nose.
InterCity 125 showing the result of fitting an air scoop over the electrical compartment to prevent fouling of nose cone by exhaust gases.

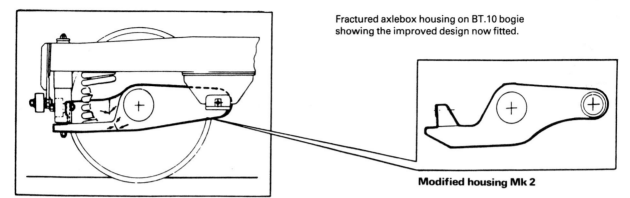

Fractured axlebox housing on BT.10 bogie
showing the improved design now fitted.

Modified housing Mk 2

Axlebox housing fracture Mk 1

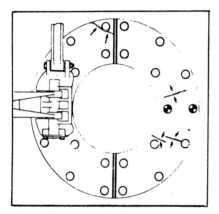

Typical types of disc fracture

Fractures in discs of brake pads.

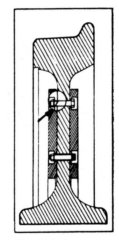

Disc bolt fracture

were taken every two days, but it is still a problem – for a reason which showed up later.

The turbocharger is the most highly stressed component in the engine, as has been illustrated by the recent application of this item to Grand Prix racing cars. The inlet temperature to the turbocharger can be up to 600°C, and with rotational speeds up to 20,000 rpm it is not surprising that there are problems. Another early problem was due to fractures in the nozzle rings; but these were overcome by a slight change in the blade shape and changing the material used to Nimonic 75.

On the transmission equipment there were a few small problems, but nothing of major significance. The designer is fortunate who can get the traction motor brushes

right first time as these are usually either too soft or too hard; too soft and the brushes need frequent changing, too hard and the commutator wears out. Since it is easier and cheaper to change brushes than to grind commutators the first option is preferred, but the brushes must not be softer than necessary. In the Brush TMH. 68-46 traction motor a split brush is used, held by a single spring resulting in unequal wear on the two halves of the brush. This was first overcome by the use of a double spring arrangement and then by a bridge piece across the two halves of the brush. The first type of short circuit protection device relied on three contacts meeting simultaneously and was prone to difficulties in adjustment. This was replaced by a single pole

device working in the exciter DC supply. Another contactor which caused trouble was the one which controlled the main exciter field; here a sticking interlock could cause the reverser to fail to respond to a driver's command when changing ends. That could cause the rear end traction motors to oppose those at the front end and at 8 mph (13 km/h) the opposing forces would bring the train to a halt. This was akin to Webb's famous compounds on the London & North Western Railway, where the high- and low-pressure cylinders could oppose each other and prevent even a start from rest.

In the maintenance depots and at certain terminus stations a shore supply is available at 415 volts to provide power for lighting, air conditioning and for battery charging so that the main engines do not have to be run to provide these services. Initially the battery charging switches tripped out when the batteries were very run down and as a result they failed to charge, but a delay device was fitted to overcome this problem.

The two worst problems still remaining concern the disc brakes and the cylinder liners on the diesel engines. In the case of the disc brakes, the discs are secured to the wheels by specially torqued bolts, two of which are of the 'fitted' type, that is an exact fit to a reamed hole. In the first design these were in the corners of the discs, but cracks started to appear in that area and the 'fitted' bolts were moved to the centre of the discs, being also enlarged to 18 mm. This has improved matters, but if cracks still occur it is a lengthy business to fit new discs and to re-ream the bolt holes every time, quite apart from the problem of stocking oversize bolts.

It is not surprising that there are problems with these brakes because the heat dissipation rate on full application works out at over 55 watts/sq cm and this can be applied several times for up to 60 seconds in the course of a journey. By way of contrast, the heating rate figure for a large jet aircraft comes out at around 350 watts/sq cm, but this is only applied once for each flight and at intervals that are several hours apart.

The problem with the cylinder liners is that of securing a perfect seal at the base of the liner and again results in water getting into the oil with the deleterious effect on the turbocharger bearings. Cast crankcases are now being tried in place of the fabricated type and this alteration should overcome the trouble. In the meantime oil samples have to be taken every other day from each engine.

One final problem, an external one, was purely aesthetic; it was caused by the exhaust from the rear power car which left a blackened patch on the driver's cab above the windscreen; this can be seen on early photographs of these trains in service. This was almost cured by fitting a deflector plate 4 in (10 cm) above the roof, and clean air is induced beneath this to form a boundary layer over the cab roof. The improvement can be seen in later photographs, but this is at the expense of blocking out the translucent panels over the electrical portion of the engine room.

We have mentioned the maintenance arrangements at the various servicing depots and a brief word might be said about the procedure when each train makes its annual visit to the main BREL workshop at Derby. This is now scheduled to take place after about 18 months or 350,000 miles (563,255 km). At Derby the train is divided and the two power cars go to the locomotive works while the coaches go to the Carriage & Wagon works at Litchurch Lane where they were first built.

The power cars are refurbished by exchanging the engine/alternator power unit for one already overhauled; at the same time the bogies are exchanged, as is the cooler group comprising the radiators, fan and drive unit. Other items exchanged are the brake module, the air compressor, the battery and the air conditioning equipment. The power car is then repainted and the pair of cars are ready for testing and rejoining

Track-recording coach with an InterCity power car to detect any misalignment of rail levels.
Right: Interior of a track-recording coach showing some of the equipment used in these measurements.

254.001 InterCity 125 set passing Selby on the East Coast main line.

Below: 254.008 InterCity 125 set passing Wetherall near Carlisle in August 1979. The station seems to be reverting to the jungle.

Top: Plasser und Theurer switch and crossing tamper, as used by British Rail for the maintenance of high-speed tracks. Plasser und Theurer PL line tamper shown alongside an InterCity 125 power car, for which it helps maintain track levels.

Below: The first production set No 253.001, approaching Wootton Bassett on the Western Region in 1980.

their carriage stock to remake the complete train.

The carriages are given similar treatment in their works with units being exchanged in the case of the bogies, the air conditioning module, the brake control module and the battery if necessary. Interior items such as carpets and seat covers are renewed and sometimes complete seats. The coaches are then given a thorough wash and clean and the skirting panels touched up where the paintwork has been damaged by pieces of ballast or other objects.

The complete overhaul takes from twenty to twenty-two working days which means that the train is away from its Region for almost six weeks, thus reducing the potential availability to 86 per cent before account is taken of any other units out of service for extended maintenance work in the running depots. If one further trainset is out of action in every dozen the availability potential is reduced to 78 per cent, and since the working diagrams call for only just under that figure there is little margin for error.

Fortunately power unit failures are of rare occurrence, but a power car or a power bogie can be put out of action by quite a small electrical fault and such items as windscreen wipers, horns and speedometers can classify a train as a failure. Trains can usually complete their journey on one power car, either pushing or pulling, but not west of Newton Abbot; no train is allowed on that section with only one engine working.

After some five years operation the ride quality in the guard's compartment at the rear end of the power car was considered unsatisfactory. While the riding in the driver's cab was very good, the rear end suffered from the interaction with the adjoining train coach. The frequency of the spring control of the two vehicles was different and this made for a very rough ride in the power car. This had been experienced in the Blue

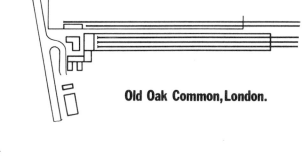

Old Oak Common, London.

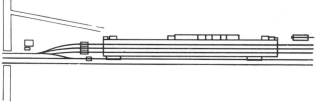

St. Philips Marsh, Bristol.

Interior of Heaton maintenance depot showing the translucent panels in the power car roof.
Plans of maintenance depots at Old Oak Common and St. Philips Marsh (Bristol).

Pullman trains, where even first class passengers were expected to ride in the power cars. This meant that the guards were unable to complete any writing or reports during the journey and they refused to do so during the running period. They had no air conditioning, unlike the driver's cab and the background noise of the power unit could be heard over the public address system when that was in use.

This lead to the leading second class coach being redesigned as a Trailer Guard Second (TGS)

InterCity 125 passing Teignmouth on Western Region

vehicle and this was put into production in 1981. These TGS vehicles were then put into the 253 and 254 train sets in place of the leading Trailer Second (TS) on a one-for-one basis; the displaced TS cars being used on new HST trains as these came into service.

A further modification is that some of the second class cars have had their seating re-arranged in line with aircraft and coach type seating, having all seats facing in the same direction. This involved the fitting of small fold-down tables in the seat backs and has enabled an additional eight seats to be accommodated in the second class coaches.

The safety record of the InterCity 125 trains has been particularly

good. There were some unusual incidents when coaches became uncoupled due to the locking pin in the alliance couplers working loose, but this has now been secured by a supplementary locking key in the actual pin. There was one case of a complete derailment on 28 August 1979 at Northallerton on the East Coast line. The 13.00 down from Kings Cross suffered from a traction motor gearbox seizure on the leading axle of the front power car due to shortage of oil. This caused a flat on the front wheels eleven inches (280 mm) long and resulted in the formation of false flanges on the outside of the wheels; when these encountered a crossover in the rails this overturned the rail and caused the derailment.

The whole train remained upright and intact due to the strength of the couplers and, although this took place at 70 mph (113 km/h), there were no casualties, and out of 450 passengers only one complained of shock. The emergency services were on the spot within five minutes of the accident.

The Present Day and Future Concepts

When the class 55 Deltics were displaced from the East Coast route by the InterCity 125 trains, there were suggestions that they might be used on the North East/South West route connecting York with Derby, Birmingham and Bristol; but their maintenance costs were getting too high and improved services on that route, known as the Heart Line, had to wait until the fourth batch of eighteen InterCity 125 sets were available. These are now working right through from Edinburgh to Penzance and will hopefully provide a useful draw to those Northerners seeking a holiday in the West of England.

These sets are of the 2 + 7 formation and although opportunities for high speed are very limited on this route, time savings of as much as two hours have been achieved between Edinburgh and Plymouth.

The final batch of 2 + 8 trains were supplied to the Eastern Region in 1981 for the services from Kings Cross to Leeds, Bradford and Harrogate. Leeds can now be reached in 130 minutes for the 186 miles (300 km) from London (85.8 mph/138 km/h).

In 1983 some of the services on the Western Region were transferred to locomotive-hauled trains to provide extra seating capacity; ten sets of their InterCity 125 trains were transferred to the former Midland line out of St Pancras to work to Sheffield via either Nottingham or Derby. These trains were also given an extra stop at Bedford to supplement the ailing diesel railcars on that route; these DMUs (class 127) had been scheduled for withdrawal from the Bedford-St Pancras services when the electric service was inaugurated, but industrial troubles delayed this for over a year and in the meantime the Bedford service was steadily deteriorating.

In October the experimental APT had carried out some high speed runs from St Pancras to Leicester, in which the time for the 99 miles (159 km) had been cut to 58 minutes. The fastest InterCity 125 now runs this journey in 72 minutes (82.5 mph/133 km/h), which is good timing for a route never laid out for high speed operation.

One result of these latest services is that Derby (the spiritual home of the High Speed Train) has at last got really good services to the North, to London and to the South West.

The latest development in the InterCity 125 story is that set No 253028 on the Western Region has just been repainted in the APT livery, with one second class and two first class coaches being provided with APT style seating. This is an executive style train for use on the routes to Bristol and South Wales and is testing public reaction to the project. It has also been described as a way of using up the seats from the abandoned APT stock, but these could have been used in the proposed new InterCity 200. A further set, No 253030, is also due to receive this treatment and may be in service in 1984.

Now that all the planned 95 sets of InterCity 125 trains are in service, what can we envisage as the next stage in the InterCity story? At present, the general pattern of passenger services on British Rail is that on those routes not served either by the electric system or by the InterCity 125, the standard locomotive-hauled main line trains made up of Mk II or Mk III stock will be the pattern for some years yet. Some branch lines can look forward hopefully to some new forms of DMU trains using either the classes 141, 150, 151 or 210, all still in the prototype stages.

Potential InterCity Electro-Diesel for use on electrified and non-electrified track.

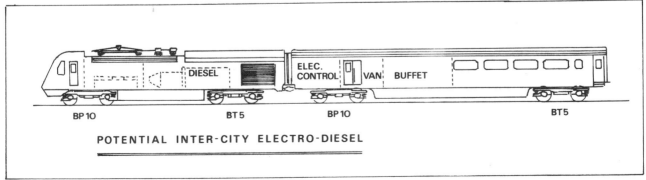

POTENTIAL INTER-CITY ELECTRO-DIESEL

Prototype electric APT outside Motherwell in 1981 prior to trials.

Road/rail co-operation. Mr Bob Reid, Chairman of British Railways Board, at that time BR's Marketing Director, and Mr Cecil Redfern, Chairman of Godfrey Davis, linking up at Paddington to sign a ten-year agreement for the Rail Drive scheme.

2 + 12 APT on trials near Beattock in 1981. The power cars are in the centre of the train.

On the West Coast main line a new form of Advanced Passenger Train is planned which will be known as the InterCity 200 or 225 or even 255. These figures represent the intended introductory maximum speed in km/hr, but the selection of this top speed depends on a number of factors which include tilting and braking. Unless the whole route is resignalled – and even realigned in many places – it does not seem that the introductory speed can be any higher than 125 mph (200 km/h), the same as the present diesel trains.

Unlike the prototype electric APT, the InterCity 200 will be based on the use of bogies similar to the BT.10 type used on the HST, which are to be known as the BT.30. These will have disc brakes and will be fitted with pads to which the tilt mechanism can be fitted. This train is proposed initially as a 2 + 10 formation to provide 499 seats and propelled by a 2,250 kW power car at each end. Its appearance will be generally similar to the prototype electric APT which was run on the West Coast line in 1981/2, but later withdrawn after the problems with the hydrokinetic brakes.

As an alternative, the Brush Electrical Engineering Company are working on a design of a Co-Co electric locomotive, intended for operation at up to 125 mph (201 km/h) and built presumably to an axle load of not more than 19 tonnes (19,000 kg). This will enable the service to be operated using the standard Mk III coaching stock, although these may be modified electrically to suit the new locomotive design.

Either of these alternatives will enable the West Coast route to compete on equal terms with their East Coast rival, but not perhaps to recapture the blue riband. There is still the problem of trains that work on both electrified and non-electrified lines. This can be overcome by working a diesel set under the wires, but this has an adverse effect on the insulators in the overhead equipment. This problem might be overcome by the use of an InterCity electro-diesel on the lines of the Southern Region class 73 locomotives; this could provide through services from Manchester and Liverpool to Scotland, as well as from London to Inverness and from Scotland to the West of England. It might involve putting some of the electrical equipment on the passenger car next to the power car, but that is nothing new. The French have produced a quadricurrant locomotive that can work on four different electrical systems and such a product should not be beyond our capability.

The InterCity 125 concept has been adapted for use in Australia by the Public Transport Commission of New South Wales, which took over the rail services in that State in October 1972. An order for ten sets of power equipment was placed with Brush Electrical Machines of Loughborough in 1980, followed by a further five sets a year later. The power cars and rolling stock were built by the Commonwealth Engineering Company (NSW) Pty Ltd at Granville and the first train was completed by September 1981. Each train consists of two power cars and five coaches, one of which is a buffet trailer having 30 seats, one has a guards compartment and 48 seats while the other three all have 72 seats. There are some fixed tables, but most seats are arranged in the aircraft style with small folding tables and all seats are first class. There is a supplementary charge over 30 miles (50 km) as well as the first class fare. The coaches are 79 feet (24.2 m) long and weigh 28 tonnes (28,000 kg) each, except for the buffet car which weighs 40 tonnes (40,000 kg).

The power cars are each 57 feet (17.35 m) long and weigh 71 tonnes (71,000 kg). The power equipment is basically the same as that for the InterCity 125, but the radiator has a greater capacity and the engine air intake is through secondary air filters to allow for the higher ambient temperatures and dust levels applicable to New South Wales. For this reason the air compressor for the brakes is fitted into the clean air compartment in the rear of the power car and two extract ventilating fans are fitted in the engine room. Since the designed top speed is 100 mph (161 km/h) the traction motor gear ratio is 65/20 compared with that of 59/23 for the InterCity 125.

The driver's cab is similar to that for the InterCity 125, but the inner skin is formed on the foam slab after this has been placed in position; this means that the mould can be lighter and only one is needed for this process. The cab's air conditioning unit is designed to cope with the air temperatures of New South Wales, while that for the passenger cars is arranged with underfloor twin compressors and with two evaporator units in the coach ceiling.

The first train set went into service in December 1981, but before that it had attained a speed of 114 mph (183 km/h) between Albury and Wagga Wagga on 6 September 1981. The operating speeds in service are at present restricted to 80 mph (129 km/h) and the routes served are from Sydney to Albury (Riverina XPT), to Canberra (Canberra XPT), to Dubbo (Central West XPT) and to Kempsey (Mid North Coast XPT).

The times and distances compared with the standard express trains are as follows:

		XPT Time	Express Time
Albury	402 miles (643 km)	7 h 20 min	8 h 55 min
Canberra	204 miles (326 km)	4 h 15 min	4 h 50 min
Dubbo	289 miles (462 km)	6 h 22 min	9 h 5 min
Kempsey	315 miles (504 km)	6 h 41 min	8 h 20 min

The single first class fares in September 1983 were:
Albury $(Aus) 4.18 plus $8 supplementary
Canberra $(Aus) 25 plus $7 supplementary
Dubbo $(Aus) 35.3 plus $8 supplementary
Kempsey $(Aus) 37.2 plus $8 supplementary

The service to Kempsey began operation in May 1982 and that to Albury in August 1982. It is hoped that, by arrangement with Vicrail of the State of Victoria, a through run from Sydney to Melbourne can be put into operation which would cut four hours off the present 13-hour journey.

High Speed Train Trial Run : 2 August 1973

Timetable, Mileages and Route Gradients

EAST COAST MAIN LINE : LONDON–DARLINGTON–LONDON

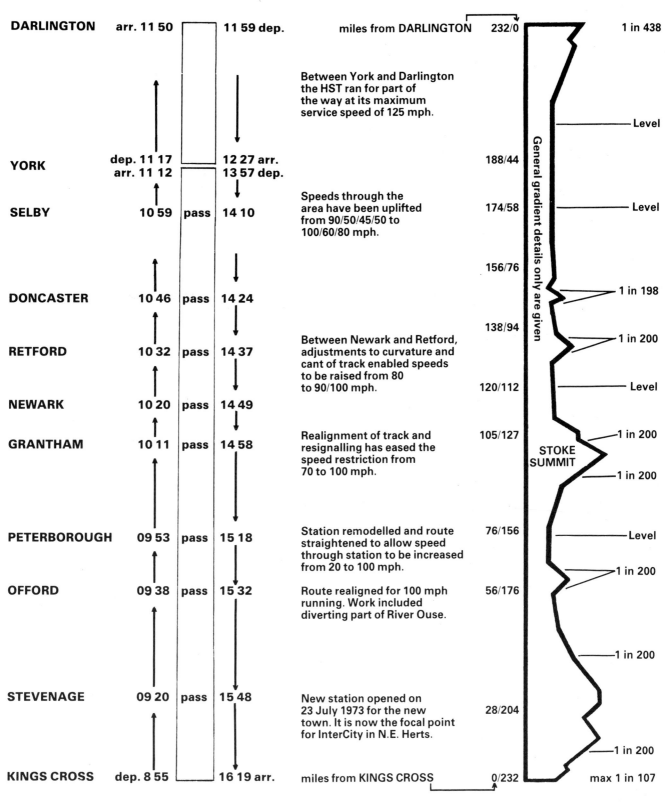

Station				Notes	miles	Gradient
DARLINGTON	arr. 11 50		11 59 dep.		miles from DARLINGTON 232/0	1 in 438
				Between York and Darlington the HST ran for part of the way at its maximum service speed of 125 mph.		Level
YORK	dep. 11 17		12 27 arr.		188/44	
	arr. 11 12		13 57 dep.			
SELBY	10 59	pass	14 10	Speeds through the area have been uplifted from 90/50/45/50 to 100/60/80 mph.	174/58	Level
					156/76	
DONCASTER	10 46	pass	14 24			1 in 198
					138/94	1 in 200
RETFORD	10 32	pass	14 37	Between Newark and Retford, adjustments to curvature and cant of track enabled speeds to be raised from 80 to 90/100 mph.		
NEWARK	10 20	pass	14 49		120/112	Level
GRANTHAM	10 11	pass	14 58	Realignment of track and resignalling has eased the speed restriction from 70 to 100 mph.	105/127	1 in 200 STOKE SUMMIT 1 in 200
PETERBOROUGH	09 53	pass	15 18	Station remodelled and route straightened to allow speed through station to be increased from 20 to 100 mph.	76/156	Level
OFFORD	09 38	pass	15 32	Route realigned for 100 mph running. Work included diverting part of River Ouse.	56/176	1 in 200
						1 in 200
STEVENAGE	09 20	pass	15 48	New station opened on 23 July 1973 for the new town. It is now the focal point for InterCity in N.E. Herts.	28/204	
						1 in 200
KINGS CROSS	dep. 8 55		16 19 arr.		miles from KINGS CROSS 0/232	max 1 in 107

General gradient details only are given

Journey Logs

1. WR: INTER-CITY 125 'JUBILEE SPECIAL'
HST unit 253 019

Drivers: A. Williams and W. J. V. Jones

Dist.		Sch.	Actual	Speeds
Miles		min.	m. s.	m.p.h.
0·00	PADDINGTON	0	0 00	—
1·20	Westbourne Park		2 29	57
2·75	Old Oak Common SB		3 48	82
5·70	Ealing Broadway		5 39	101
9·05	Southall	8½	7 29	114
13·20	West Drayton		9 34	124
18·40	SLOUGH	13	12 01	128
24·20	Maidenhead	16	14 46	126
30·95	Twyford	19	17 57	128
35·95	READING	21½	20 28	76*
38·60	Tilehurst		22 18	97
44·70	Goring		25 35	122
53·10	DIDCOT	31	29 33	128/125
63·35	Challow (boundary)	36	34 23	128
71·45	Shrivenham		38 14	127
77·25	SWINDON	43	41 12	98*/115
83·05	Wootton Bassett Junc.	46½	44 34	66*
86·95	Brinkworth		47 08	104
94·20	Hullavington	53	50 51	120
99·95	Badminton		53 52	111*/116
107·10	Westerleigh Junc.	60	57 44	102/113
111·75	BRISTOL PARKWAY	62½	60 36	50*
112·80	Filton		61 45	55/71
115·95	Stapleton Road		64 42	52*
117·60	BRISTOL TEMPLE MEADS	70	67 35	—

*Speed restrictions. Average speed 104·4 m.p.h.

2. WR: INTER-CITY 125 'JUBILEE SPECIAL', MAY 7, 1977
HST unit 253 019

Drivers: W. H. Francis and R. J. Sandercock

Dist.		Sch.	Actual	Speeds
Miles		min.	m. s.	m.p.h.
0·0	BRISTOL TEMPLE MEADS	0	0 00	—
1·6	Stapleton Road	3½	2 48	—
3·7	Horfield		4 52	74
4·8	Filton Junc.		5 51	50*
5·9	BRISTOL PARKWAY	8	7 02	—
7·7	Winterbourne		8 40	—
10·4	Westerleigh Junc.	11½	10 26	97
13·0	Chipping Sodbury		11 56	110
17·6	Badminton		14 30	115/110
23·4	Hullavington	18½	17 25	125
27·9	Little Somerford		19 34	125
30·6	Brinkworth		20 59	100
34·7	Wootton Bassett	24½	23 50	68*
37·6	Milepost 80		25 50	112
40·3	SWINDON	28½	27 21	100*
43·9	Milepost 73¾		29 20	112
46·1	Shrivenham		30 27	123
51·1	Uffington		32 52	125
53·7	Challow	35½	34 07	125
57·2	Wantage Road		35 48	125
61·1	Steventon		37 41	124
64·5	DIDCOT	40½	39 18	126
69·1	Cholsey		41 30	125
73·8	Goring		43 18	126
76·1	Pangbourne		44 51	126
78·9	Tilehurst		46 14	120
81·6	READING	49	48 00	80*
83·6	Milepost 34		49 18	101
86·6	Twyford		50 57	116
90·6	Milepost 27		52 55	125
93·4	Maidenhead	55½	54 46	127
96·6	Burnham		55 46	126
99·1	SLOUGH	58½	56 57	126
101·4	Langley		58 02	127
104·4	West Drayton		59 26	127
108·5	SOUTHALL	63	61 25	127
110·2	Hanwell		62 14	124
111·9	Ealing Broadway		63 02	126
114·4	Old Oak West Junc.		64 34	—
115·6	Milepost 2		65 28	—
116·3	Westbourne Park		66 04	—
117·6	PADDINGTON	70½	68 23	—

*Speed restrictions. Average speed 103·3 m.p.h.

3. BRITISH RAILWAYS: WR, 09.20 HST: PADDINGTON-CHIPPENHAM, APRIL 10, 1979

Dist.		Sch.	Actual	Speeds
Miles		min.	m. s.	m.p.h.
0·00	PADDINGTON	0	0 00	—
1·25	Milepost 1¼		2 36	—
2·00	Milepost 2		3 14	71·1
3·25	Milepost 3¼		4 10	80·6
5·70	Ealing Broadway		5 37	—
6·00	Milepost 6		5 48	100·9
7·50	Milepost 7½		6 36	112·5
9·00	Southall (MP9)	8½	7 21	120·0
11·00	Milepost 11		8 19	124·0
13·25	West Drayton		9 24	124·5
16·25	Langley		10 50	125·4
18·50	SLOUGH	13	11 55	124·5
21·00	Burnham		13 07	125·0
24·20	Maidenhead	16	14 39	125·0
27·00	Milepost 27		16 00	124·4
29·00	Milepost 29		16 57	126·2
31·00	Twyford	19	17 54	126·2
33·00	Milepost 33		18 52	124·1
35·00	Milepost 35		19 51	122·2
36·00	READING	21½	20 33	85·8
38·50	Milepost 38½		22 15	88·3
41·50	Pangbourne		23 54	109·0
44·75	Goring		25 29	123·0
48·50	Cholsey		27 18	123·4
51·50	Milepost 51½		28 45	124·0
53·10	DIDCOT	31	29 31	—
56·50	Steventon		31 09	124·8
60·50	Milepost 60½		33 04	124·8
—	(Boundary 63·35)	36	—	—
64·00	Milepost 64		34 45	124·8
66·50	Uffington		35 57	125·0
69·00	Milepost 69		37 08	126·3
71·50	Shrivenham		38 20	125·0
73·75	Milepost 73¾		39 25	124·5
76·00	Milepost 76		40 36	114·0
77·30	SWINDON	47½	41 24	97·6
80·00	Milepost 80		42 57	104·3
83·00	Wootton Bassett (MP83)	51	44 27	120·0
85·00	Milepost 85		45 25	124·2
87·75	Dauntsey		46 45	123·8
91·00	Milepost 91		48 18	125·8
92·75	Milepost 92¾		49 10	121·0
94·00	CHIPPENHAM	57½	50 32	—

Note: 4½ min. recovery time Challow–Swindon

4. THE DOWN 'CORNISH RIVIERA EXPRESS'

Load to Westbury   14 cars 492/525 tons
    to Taunton   12 cars 421/450 tons
    to Exeter   10 cars 357/380 tons
    to Plymouth   7 cars 253/270 tons

Engine: No. 6011 King James I

Driver: Wright   Fireman: Hounslow

Dist.		Sch.	Actual	Speeds
Miles		min.	m. s.	m.p.h.
0·0	PADDINGTON	0	0 00	—
1·3	Westbourne Park		3 05	—
5·7	Ealing		9 10	—
9·1	SOUTHALL	11	12 45	59
13·2	West Drayton		16 55	65
18·5	SLOUGH	20	21 35	70½
24·2	Maidenhead	25½	26 40	66
36·0	READING	37	37 30	slack 40
44·8	Aldermaston		46 55	65
53·1	NEWBURY	55½	54 55	61
58·5	Kintbury		60 10	62½
61·5	Hungerford		63 15	57½/61½
66·4	Bedwyn	68½	68 15	58½
68·6	Grafton Curve Junc.		70 50	p.w.s. 20
70·1	Savernake		73 55	
75·3	Pewsey		79 05	71½
81·1	Patney		83 50	77½/80½
86·9	Lavington		88 35	p.w.s. 20
95·6	WESTBURY	96	98 35	slack 35
98·5	Milepost 112¾		102 05	54
101·3	FROME		105 30	slack 35
106·6	Witham		112 00	53½
108·5	Milepost 122¾		114 15	50½
111·9	Bruton		117 15	77½/83½
115·3	CASTLE CARY	118	120 00	slack 50
120·2	Keinton Mandeville		124 55	67
125·7	Somerton		129 45	75
131·0	Curry Rivell Junc.		134 05	79
137·9	Cogload Junc.	140	140 55	p.w.s. 10
142·9	TAUNTON	144½	147 45	58½
144·9	Norton Fitzwarren		149 45	62½
147·5	Milepost 167¾		152 10	64
150·0	Wellington		154 40	58½
152·8	Milepost 173		157 55	42½
153·8	Whiteball Box		159 25	44
158·8	Tiverton Junc.		164 05	76½
161·1	Cullompton		165 55	80½
170·2	Stoke Canon		173 05	76½
173·7	EXETER	174½	175 50	70
178·4	Exminster		179 40	82
				p.w.s. 10
188·7	Teignmouth		195 25	slack 40/45
193·9	NEWTON ABBOT	198½	201 25	slack 25
195·7	Milepost 216		204 13	50½
197·7	Dainton Box	204½	207 50	24½/60
202·5	Totnes	210½	213 35	53
204·7	Milepost 225		216 49	31½
205·3	Tigley Box		217 50	29
207·1	Rattery Box		221 15	36
209·4	Brent	219½	224 10	54
211·6	Wrangaton		226 40	p.w.s. 25
219·0	Hemerdam Box	231	235 55	60/68
221·7	Plympton		238 30	50
225·4	Mutley		sigs.	
225·7	PLYMOUTH	240	245 35	

Net times, Paddington to Exeter   167¾ min.
Paddington to Plymouth   228 min.

Reproduced by permission of the *Railway Magazine*.

5. WR: PADDINGTON-EXETER

Date: July 4, 1983
HST: formation/power car Nos.   2+7/43131/43007
Load: No./empty/full (tons) 7/374/390

Dist.		Sch.	Actual	Speeds
Miles		min.	m. s.	m.p.h.
0·0	PADDINGTON	0	0 00	—
5·6	Ealing Broadway	6	5 30	102
9·0	Southall	8	7 21	120
10·8	Hayes		8 18	125
13·1	West Drayton		9 25	125
			sigs.	—*
18·3	SLOUGH	12	13 14	90
			sigs.	—*
24·1	MAIDENHEAD	15	16 41	90*
30·9	Twyford	18	21 21	109/
				101*
			sig.	
		[1]	stop	—
35·9	READING	22	28 12	31
37·6	Southcote Junc.	24	30 31	73
41·2	Theale		32 47	102
46·6	Midgham		36 04	100
			sigs.	40*
49·4	Thatcham		38 35	58
53·0	Newbury	34	41 15	99
58·4	Kintbury		44 43	92/75*
61·4	Hungerford		47 11	85/60*
66·3	Bedwyn	43	50 56	92/60*
75·2	Pewsey		57 35	92
78·8	Woodborough	52	59 54	95
			p.w.s.	20*
86·8	Lavington	59	67 49	95/102
92·9	Milepost 93	[2]	71 30	101
94·5	Heywood Road Junc.	65	72 37	75*
96·9	Fairwood Junc.	67	74 26	82
100·2	Clink Road Junc.	69	76 45	90/81*
102·2	Blatchbridge Junc.	70	78 15	81*/90
106·3	Witham		81 07	93
111·6	Bruton		84 53	75*/94
115·1	CASTLE CARY	80	87 13	92/75*
119·9	Keinton Mandeville		90 26	97/90*
125·4	Somerton		94 13	88
129·6	Langport East	[1]	96 59	93
134·7	Athelney		100 17	95
137·8	Cogload Junc.		102 21	91/84*
142·6	TAUNTON	100	106 04	70*/80
149·7	Wellington		110 55	85*/90
153·4	Whiteball Siding	108	113 28	86/95
158·6	Tiverton Junc.		116 53	95/80*
160·8	Cullompton	[1]	118 23	92/76*
170·0	Stoke Canon		124 41	92
			sigs.	48*
172·1	Cowley Bridge Junc.	121	126 38	45
173·4	EXETER ST. DAVIDS	123	129 01	—

*Speed restrictions

6. WR: EXETER-PLYMOUTH 'CORNISH RIVIERA EXPRESS' HST

Dist.		Sch.	Actual	Speeds
Miles		min.	m. s.	m.p.h.
0.0	EXETER	0	0 00	—
4·8	Exminster		4 35	90/55*
8·5	Starcross		7 32	66
10·5	Dawlish Warren	9½	9 12	77
12·2	Dawlish		10 39	60*/67
15·0	Teignmouth		13 22	54*
—			—	82
20·1	NEWTON ABBOT	18½	18 33	40*
22·1	Milepost 216		21 24	55
24·1	Dainton Box	23½	23 42	48/50
28·9	TOTNES	29	28 50	60 (max)
				52*
31·1	Milepost 225		31 13	57
33·6	Milepost 227½		33 58	46*
35·7	Brent	36½	36 08	64/57
37·9	Wrangaton		38 18	64/61
			sigs.	38
41·2	Ivybridge		44 10	60
45·3	Hemerdon	46	45 55	—
48·1	Milepost 242		48 07	80
50·5	Lipson Junc.		50 16	—
—			sigs.	—
52·0	PLYMOUTH NORTH RD.	53	53 06	—

*Speed restrictions

Power Car Specification

Wheel arrangement:	Bo-Bo
Diesel engine:	Paxman 'Valenta' 12RP 200L
Power output:	2250 hp or 1680 kW at 1500 rpm
Main alternator:	Brush 1468 kW at 1500 rpm
Traction motors:	Four Brush TMH68-46 467 hp
Braking system:	Davies & Metcalfe E 70 Electrically-controlled air-brake on Girling discs on all wheels
Air compressor:	Davies & Metcalfe 2A115 two-stage
Bogie wheelbase:	2.6 m
Overall length:	17.79 m
Overall weight:	70 tonnes
Overall height:	3.906 m
Overall width:	2.74 m
Fuel tank capacity:	5,680 litres
Train auxiliary supplies:	415V 50 Hz 3 phase
Acceleration on level track:	70 mph: 2.1 mins
	100 mph: 4.5 mins
	110 mph: 6.0 mins
	120 mph: 9.0 mins
	125 mph: 11.5 mins
Maximum speed attained:	143 mph
Wheel diameter:	1.02 m

Acknowledgements

The author would like to thank the following for their help in supplying illustrations:

Metro-Cammel Ltd, Birmingham, (Mr. M. Botham): p. 8 (both).
Paxman Diesels Ltd, Colchester, (Mr. Youldon): pp. 21 (bottom), 25, 26 (top).
Brush Electrical Machines Ltd, Loughborough, (Mr. D. Mays): pp. 20 (bottom), 26 (centre and bottom), 30-31.
Plasser Railway Machinery (GB) Ltd, London: p. 47 (top and centre).
Railway Magazine, Mr. O. S. Nock, and Mr. P. W. B. Semmens for the journey logs on pages 55/56.
Mr. P. Underhay: pp. 17 (bottom), 19, 20 (top), 21 (top), 22 (top), 24 (bottom).
British Rail, Rail House, London, (Mr. D. A. Marshall) for most other illustrations.